METAL **'s**

METAL heads

HEAVY METAL
MUSIC AND
ADOLESCENT ALIENATION

Jeffrey Jensen Arnett

WestviewPress
A Division of HarperCollins*Publishers*

Copyright © 1996 by Westview Press, Inc., A Division of HarperCollins Publishers, Inc.

Published in 1996 in the United States of America by Westview Press, Inc., 5500 Central
Avenue, Boulder, Colorado, 80301-2877, and in the United Kingdom by Westview Press, 12
Hid's Copse Road, Cumnor Hill, Oxford OX2 9JJ

Library of Congress Cataloging-in-Publication Data
Arnett, Jeffrey Jensen.
  Metalheads : heavy metal music and adolescent alienation / Jeffrey Jensen
Arnett.
     p.   cm.
  Includes bibliographical references (p.   ) and index.
  ISBN 0-8133-2812-8 (hardcover)—ISBN 0-8133-2813-6 (paperback)
    1. Youth—United States.   2. Alienation (Social psychology)—
United States.   3. Subculture—United States.   4. Heavy metal
(Music)—United States.   I. Title.
HQ796.A726   1996
305.23'5'0973—dc20   95-45689
                                                                      CIP

The paper used in this publication meets the requirements of the American National
Standard for Permanence of Paper for Printed Library Materials Z39-1984.

10   9   8   7   6   5   4   3   2   1

contents

tables and photographs

Tables

Photographs

preface

I was first inspired to study the fans of heavy metal music by a student of mine. At the time I was an assistant professor at a small liberal arts college in Atlanta, teaching several courses and beginning some research on adolescence. One of the classes I taught at the college was Introductory Psychology, and one day after class I got to talking with a student named Henry. At some point I had mentioned my research interests in adolescence and at another point my musical interests (I play guitar and piano). Henry saw the possible intersection of the two before I did. "You should go to a heavy metal concert," he said. "If you're interested in adolescents, you should see this. Besides, the music's great."

I expressed my skepticism about his assessment of the music, but I was intrigued by what he had to say about it. It interested me that he should be such an avid "metalhead" (as heavy metal fans call themselves). He did not conform to the metalhead stereotype: scruffy-looking, sneering, apathetic. On the contrary, he was always well groomed, nicely dressed, polite, and respectful. He was also one of the brightest students I had ever taught. What did a guy like him find so appealing about heavy metal? Over the course of many conversations, I learned the answer.

A few weeks after my first conversation with Henry, the heavy metal band Metallica came to town, and I was able to get a free ticket through a friend of mine who was running the concessions for the show. It was an amazing spectacle, as reflected both in the zealousness of the fans and the violence of the music. I found it fascinating and also disturbing in some respects. I came away from it determined to do a study of metalheads and their subculture.

The study involved over 100 metalheads, including 70 boys and 38 girls.[1] The boys were interviewed in suburban Atlanta, Georgia, and the girls in Atlanta and in Cambridge, Massachusetts. However, they had grown up in diverse places all over the country. To find the metalheads, I put up a sign in a music store describing the study and offering a free cassette tape of their choice in return for their participation. I conducted all the interviews for the boys; female research assistants interviewed the girls. The interviews lasted anywhere from twenty minutes to over two hours.

Some metalheads were reticent, but most were eager to talk not just about heavy metal but about every aspect of their lives. As the interviews accumulated, I was struck again and again by the depth and pervasiveness of their alienation. Most of them held high hopes for their own lives, but they were deeply cynical about the adult world they were preparing to enter. Few of them had reliable and gratifying ties to family, school, community, or religion. Most of their lives were characterized by radical individualism, taken to such an extreme that they had little sense of obligation or attachment to others. Many of them were proud of this, and they jealously asserted their self-sufficiency and their right to do whatever they pleased as long as it did not directly harm anyone else. At the same time, however, it was clear that many of them were angry or lonely much of the time. Soon the focus of my interest had changed from the effects of heavy metal music on adolescents to what their love for the music reflects about their alienation and, more generally, about adolescent alienation in the United States. This alienation became the central topic of the book.

The metalheads in the study were 13–25 years old[2] (average age 17.6 for the boys, 18.4 for the girls). There were 31 questions in the interview, shown in the Appendix. I also had them fill out several questionnaires. Once the information on the metalheads was collected, I compared their responses on the interviews and questionnaires to the responses of 118 adolescent boys who preferred other kinds of music. I recruited most of the boys (94 of them) for this comparison group of adolescents through classrooms in a local high school, but I also included 24 male students from college classes of mine in order to make the age range of the comparison group similar to the age range for the metalheads.[3] I also collected questionnaire data from 199 girls who were not heavy metal fans for comparison with the female metalheads. Chapter 8 describes the results of the interviews with the girls.

I have avoided rehashing the public debate over heavy metal. Readers interested in that debate can find accounts in books by Deanna Weinstein (1991) and Robert Walser (1993). Also, though I present a song analysis in Chapter 3, a more detailed analysis of the musical properties of particular heavy metal songs can be found in Walser's book. My primary interest is not the music but the fans: what the music means to them and what it reflects about their lives.

The book is based on my interviews with the metalheads, along with many other informal conversations I have had with metalheads, as well as my experiences in attending heavy metal concerts and listening to heavy metal cassettes. However, this book is about not only the heavy metal subculture but adolescence in contemporary America, using the voices of the metalheads to illustrate various points. Throughout the book I use information from national studies and national statistics to discuss various characteristics of American youth, then use the material from my interviews with the metalheads to bring these other studies and statistics to life. This is not to say that metalheads are no different from adolescents who prefer other types of music. As comparisons throughout the book will show, in some respects they are quite different. But some of the most disturbing trends among American adolescents—the alienation, the cynicism, the recklessness—are illustrated with particular vividness in the lives of the metalheads.

Why does the book focus mostly on boys, with the exception of the one chapter devoted to girls? There are two reasons. One is that the heavy metal subculture is largely male: Go to a concert and you see almost all adolescent boys, aged 13–25.[4] Girls make up maybe 10 percent of the crowd. In the surveys I have done in high school classrooms, too, heavy metal is much more popular among boys than among girls.[5] Second, many of the most serious problems of contemporary adolescents—suicide and automobile fatalities, to give two examples—are more severe among boys than among girls.[6] Some adolescent girls do like heavy metal, and some adolescent girls have serious problems, but in this book I have chosen to focus on the boys because heavy metal mainly reflects them and their concerns. (I refer to them as "boys" throughout the book, even though some of them are well beyond boyhood, so as to avoid having to use the awkward "boys/young men" every time. The reader should keep in mind the age range, 13–25.)

I am grateful to a number of people for their advice and assistance during the time I have been writing this book. Reed Larson, Keith Roe, and Claudia Steinbrecher all provided useful comments and suggestions on the manuscript. Helena Stauber and Csilla Csizar conducted most of the interviews with the girls. Gordon Massman of Westview Press provided helpful editorial advice and encouragement. Freelance editor Jon Taylor Howard did a terrific job of copyediting. Oglethorpe University and the University of Missouri provided research funding. Most valuable of all has been the contribution of my wife, Lene Jensen, who has read the manuscript at numerous stages and each time provided an insightful critique.

Perhaps I should offer a confession or a disclaimer with regard to my opinion of the music itself. I love many kinds of music, but heavy metal is not one of them. In fact, one of the reasons I became interested in it was that I was amazed that anyone could find it appealing, and that made me want to find out why they did. Attending many heavy metal concerts and listening to dozens of tapes has failed to convert me. Still, I think I understand quite well by now the appeal heavy metal music holds for the metalheads, and I respect the love that they have for it and the importance it holds in their lives.

Jeffrey Jensen Arnett

Jack

Jack had a striking appearance. His hair was straight and long, past his shoulders, and blond, sun-soaked from long summer hours of working construction outdoors. His skin was tanned baseball-glove brown, and he had a brownish beard of perhaps two weeks' growth. He was wearing a blue tie-dyed halter t-shirt and old blue jeans, with huge holes in the knees, nearly worn through on the left thigh.

The most striking things about him, however, were his jewelry and tattoos. He wore an earring in each ear—in his right ear a person hanging from a noose, in his left, a crucifix. Another crucifix dangled as a necklace, and on his left hand he sported a tattoo of yet another.

The crosses decorating his body did not signify devoutness on his part. "It's just something I like," he said. He also had a tattoo of a black rose on his left arm. This had a more explainable (if somewhat bizarre) significance to him. "I love roses," he said. "I love them when they die. I got a big old goldfish jar with black rose petals that I've kept over the years. When I was in treatment [for drug abuse], my girlfriend used to send me black roses every week. And they [the hospital personnel] would say that's real morbid and everything. When I die, I want twenty-one dozen black roses on my coffin."

He had had a tough and chaotic life so far, this eighteen-year-old who was already thinking about how he wanted his coffin to be decorated. His past included a tumultuous relationship with his father, dropping out of high school at age sixteen, a stay in a psychiatric hospital for drug abuse, and time in jail for auto theft and breaking and entering. He was highly reckless in the present, too; his Summary Profile (see below) shows his history of high-speed and drunk driving, high-risk sexual behavior, and drug use over the past year. His alienation was deep—he was estranged from his father, and he said he admired no one, had no interest in politics or religion, and had no idea what to do with his life. There may have been a yearning for meaning in his attraction to crosses and black roses—and to heavy metal music. Unlike most things in

1

life, heavy metal is "something no one can take away from you," he said. "You can take away a lot of things from people but you can't really take away music, 'cause that's your own. Ain't nobody ever gonna come into my house and take my tapes."

The music clearly had an ideological significance for him. That was why he had volunteered to be in the study, to "defend our music, talk to people, let them see that it's not what they think." To him, the dark music and pessimistic lyrics of heavy metal songs reflect the harsh reality of life.

> I have a hard time with all these people that put down [heavy metal bands] and say they're satanic and they worship the devil and all this. If you listen to the words in their songs, it's all reality. Dying is reality, nuclear war is reality, going out and killing somebody is reality, living on the streets is reality, and they talk about reality problems.

But the sheer intensity of the music, and the pleasure and excitement of that intensity, were also part of the attraction for him. "The music is so powerful, it's so strong, it's real energizing," he said. "You put the music on and it gets you in a better mood and gets you moving. . . . It's real intense, real intense." Listening to it with friends added to the excitement and intensity of it for him. He enjoyed getting together to slamdance with them—jostling, colliding, and slamming into each other, arms flailing, legs pumping, and bodies convulsing or careening while the heavy metal music plays.

> It's fun to just crawl into one room with nothing in it—nothing but a little stereo—and throw on some wild music. Get about fifteen people in a small room and start slamdancing, basically beating the hell out of each other. But we can hit each other and knock each other on the ground and everything and we just turn around and look at each other and say, "What's up man? Help me up." No big deal. It's just because it's all in fun.

Jack spoke glowingly of the experience of attending heavy metal concerts and the exhilarating sense of being united there with fellow metalheads. "It's great to go with a bunch of friends and just get wild," he said. "Whenever you get 10,000 headbangers in a room you don't want to piss us off, you don't want to get in our way." He also spoke of the concert setting as a place to expel his problems. "To me, at a concert, that's your time, it's your place, to release yourself from all the anxiety and troubles."

He relied a great deal on heavy metal, on a daily basis. "I listen to my music every single day. It's an addiction to me," he said. "If I go without it, I miss it." His use of the word "addiction" was more than a metaphor; he said he had used the music as a substitute for his former drug addiction. "You can get the same feeling just from the music. I mean, I can listen to a song and it can put me in a better mood than smoking a joint or doing some drugs or something. I used to have a pretty bad drug problem, and the music has helped me stay away from it." Nevertheless, as his Summary Profile indicates, his drug problem persisted at the time we spoke.

Although the music was a source of fun for him in slamdancing and attending concerts, and he used it to induce the kind of pleasurable feelings he associated with drug use, it also seemed to signify a reservoir of anger. For Jack, as for many of the other metalheads, the music was an expression of anger—and a way of purging it.

I can be real mad—there's been a lot of times I've been real mad—and I can listen to a tape and it's calmed me down. I mean I've gotten all my feelings and all my anger out through the music, listening to it instead of me going out and bashing somebody's head in or going out and just raising a bunch of hell. It's a release.

Why was he so angry? Like many metalheads in the study, Jack saw the world as a bleak and corrupt place and was deeply alienated from it, deeply pessimistic about the future of it. Also like many metalheads, Jack's anger also had a source closer to home—in his family life. For Jack, the deepest source was his anguished and alienated relationship with his father. When Jack was younger, father and son had a "close, close relationship." They shared the enjoyment of playing baseball and football and of riding motorcycles. As Jack entered adolescence, however, his father suddenly began working long hours and was rarely home. "All of a sudden I didn't have him there any more, and it hurt," said Jack. "That's why I still have a lot of anger toward him, because I miss him a lot. My parents are divorced now and I haven't talked to my dad in probably three or four months. And I miss that closeness."

The remoteness of his father and the resulting anger toward his father had contributed to making Jack's adolescence an exceptionally reckless one. Jack said that one reason for stealing, using drugs, and staying out late as an adolescent was "just to get his [father's] attention." Still, anger toward his father was not Jack's only motivation for his recklessness. He enjoyed it, for the same reason he enjoyed heavy metal music—the sheer excitement of it, the sensation-seeking intensity of it. By age fifteen he had broken into dozens of people's homes and stolen thirty-four automobiles. Why?

> I could get away with it. I was good at it. The intensity of being in someone else's room when they're sleeping, taking their jewelry, their money, and their car keys, right there while they're sleeping in the bed, and you're looking right over them. . . . It was real intense, it was a rush. You know, "What can you get away with? How far can you push your limit?" I found out.

The experience of spending time in juvenile jail for theft and then in a psychiatric hospital for drug abuse had changed him, made him less reckless, he said. But he remained highly reckless compared to most people his age—or any age, for that matter. He may have progressed from out of control to barely in control, but he still seemed headed for trouble. In his eyes the future held little promise worth preserving himself for. When I asked him what he saw himself doing in ten years, he had trouble envisioning anything at all. "I don't know. I don't look that far ahead," he said. "My head spins if I do. That's when you start looking at depression. I'm like, 'What am I going to do in life?' you know what I mean? I just stick with today, that's just the way it goes."

The upheavals of Jack's young life had made him feel wounded and wary, perhaps permanently. His alienation was so deep by this time that it may have become a permanent part of him. It is no wonder that he identified so strongly with the angry, lonely, defiant heroes of heavy metal songs; he, too, was angry, lonely, and defiant.

> I've been hurt a lot, walked on, told this, told that, a lot of false promises, and I don't like it at all. That's why I really don't trust no-

body. I don't think I'm ever going to get anywhere or make anything of myself without doing it myself. I keep Jack pretty locked up for right now as far as feelings and letting anybody in to touch me. It's been a long life.

Summary profile: Jack

Age: 18
Race: White
Education: quit school at age sixteen
Current occupation: construction worker
Father's occupation: telephone company middle-management
Mother's occupation: child care worker
Family background: parents divorced two months ago, father remote and often absent beginning when Jack was twelve years old
Spent most of childhood in: Florida
Number of heavy metal recordings owned: over 300
Favorite heavy metal groups: Mötley Crüe, Metallica, Megadeth
Goals in ten years: "I don't look that far ahead"
Political orientation: "I don't know"
Religious orientation: atheist
Hobbies/leisure preferences: plays electric guitar, sang in heavy metal band for three years
Three people most admired: "Me, myself, and I"
Number of times in past year:

Driven a car under the influence of alcohol:	>10
Driven a car over 80 miles per hour:	>50
Driven a car greater than 20 mph over speed limit:	>50
Had sex without contraception:	>10
Had sex with someone not known well:	>10
Used marijuana:	>10
Used cocaine:	>10
Used illegal drugs other than marijuana or cocaine:	2–5
Damaged or destroyed public or private property:	0
Shoplifted:	0

1

A Heavy Metal Concert:
The Sensory Equivalent of War

Heavy metal is, as much as anything else, an arena of gender, where spectacular gladiators compete to register and affect ideas of masculinity, sexuality, and gender.

—heavy metal scholar Robert Walser, *Running with the Devil*

The death of a culture begins when its normative institutions fail to communicate ideals in ways that remain inwardly compelling. . . . At the breaking point, a culture can no longer maintain itself as an established span of moral demands. Its jurisdiction contracts; it demands less, permits more. Bread and circuses become confused with right and duty. Spectacle becomes a functional substitute for sacrament.

—Philip Rieff, *The Triumph of the Therapeutic*

You must wait in line to enter the concert arena, along with the pilgrims. There are several lines leading into the arena, but every person who enters must be frisked to make sure he is not attempting to smuggle in alcohol or photography equipment. It is quite cold outside, being early March in the Midwest, but few people seem to mind. Their thoughts are on the spectacle to come and on past spectacles. You hear their comments. "Did you see these guys last year?" someone says, presumably referring to the headline act for the evening, the heavy metal band Iron Maiden. "It was great!" His companion says regretfully that he missed that show, but he offers similar praise for a Metallica concert he attended.

Most of the concertgoers waiting to enter are young males (about 90 percent of the crowd), in their teens and early twenties. You see a few who look younger, surprisingly young, perhaps nine or ten years old, and a few others who are clearly adults, middle-aged. Some of these adults you will recognize later on during the show, reading, smoking, and chatting in the lobby, avoiding the noise to the extent possible and waiting to escort their children home.

At last you enter the lobby, which is warm with activity. The action is centered around the concession stands, where t-shirts ($18–20), programs ($10), and other items bearing the logos of Iron Maiden or Anthrax are being sold. The young "metalheads" (as they call themselves; also known as

Dressed to thrill at a heavy metal concert. (Photo by Nick Romanenko)

"headbangers") press forward eagerly, awaiting their chance to purchase one or more of the tokens displayed there.

You move through the lobby and find your reserved seat, about thirty rows up. From the looks of the sound system, you should have no problem hearing the bands. It is evident that the metalheads have come to exalt not only performers and music tonight but volume, sheer volume. There are twenty raised speakers on each side of the stage, plus ten five-foot-high speakers sitting on each side, and ten more sitting center stage. These are, undoubtedly, the best speakers that money can buy, designed with breathtaking technological sophistication. Any one of them alone would probably be sufficient to fill even this enormous arena with sound.

People are filing in gradually and taking their seats. Not much is happening so far. "Heavy fucking metal!" a beer-swilling, mesomorphic young man of about twenty years old shouts periodically. Two boys near the front of the stage hold up an American flag, to loud cheers. Two other boys in the vicinity hold up another American flag, this time with the Iron Maiden logo in place of the field of stars, to louder cheers.

The girls are noticeable as they walk in to find their seats, not only because they are distinctly in the minority, but because many of them are dressed in highly suggestive clothing. The nature of this suggestion is not lost on the boys around them. One girl walks down the aisle wearing a dress better suited for prom night than a heavy metal concert. It is deep red, with bare shoulders, a mostly bare back, and a low neckline. Wolf whistles, predatory stares, and derisive smiles follow her as she goes.

Other girls wear clothes that are not only suggestive but downright obscene. One girl who walks by you in the lobby is wearing a blue spandex top with no bra. The top button of her faded jeans is open, and the zipper is down about two inches. She has a blank, addled look on her face. Another girl is wearing a bright purple dress with large oval spaces on each side revealing her flesh (and the absence of underwear) all the way up to her waist. She, like many of the other girls, is laden with makeup. But not all of the girls are dressed in this neoprostitute style. Many are dressed like the boys, in the trademark metalhead style of denim jeans, a black "concert" t-shirt bearing the logo of a heavy metal band, and a leather or denim jacket.

Some metalheads also wear these clothes for occasions other than concerts, and their dress marks them off as different from peers at school. It is their declaration of identity as a metalhead/headbanger.[1] But there is a certain conformity in their nonconformity: The standard dress is the black t-shirt, worn-out jeans, and jacket. Still, not everyone at the concert is dressed that way; many of them look like they could be at a basketball game or a party.

At last the crowd has filled the seats and the concert seems about to begin. The first band to take the stage is Anthrax, named after the cattle disease. Their stage prop is a clock with skulls at three, six, and nine o'clock, red lights for the eyes of the skulls, and the bones of a human skeleton shaping the number twelve and serving as the minute and hour hands. The hands of the clock begin to move, and the band takes the stage. The crowd roars in greeting. The lead singer of the band shouts a greeting in return, and the concert begins.

The volume of the sound that follows is stunning, even for those who are prepared for it. On occasion you can actually feel your ribcage vibrating. The musical emphasis is on volume, power, and intensity, whereas melody and harmony are virtually absent. It is a cacophony in rhythm; virtually all you can hear is the beat being pounded out by the drums and the bass guitar, and the singer's voice screeching something unintelligible. Although there are two electric guitar players, you can hardly hear the electric guitars at all. You certainly cannot hear individual notes.

Whatever an unbeliever might think of it as music, the metalheads appear to be enjoying it thoroughly. Often they sing along on the chorus, indicating their prior familiarity with the songs. As you look around you can see their faces intermittently lit up by the reflected light from the stage. When they are not singing along, many of them have a mesmerized look about them, mouths open, sometimes a slight smile. Virtually all of them remain on their feet through the entire performance.

Down on the floor of the arena a commotion is taking place. The fans there have cleared out the chairs to form a dancing "pit" about twenty-five feet in diameter. (Pits are de rigueur at metal concerts; they are sometimes referred to as a "slamdancing pit" or "mosh pit.") In it there are bodies crashing into one another, and the more you watch the more it becomes apparent that they are doing this deliberately, in a violent dance. This is what metalheads call "moshing" or "slamdancing." They often slam against one another so hard that one or both of them end up on the floor. After one especially forceful collision you see a boy put his hand to his head as he pulls himself up from the floor. He appears to be bleeding, but he is smiling in a pained way. Is he smiling in spite of, or *because* of, his injury?

A battalion of security guards moves into the slamdancing pit and soon restores order of a sort. Attention returns to the stage. The band is performing with great energy, the drummer thrashing relentlessly in every direction, the guitar players and singer jumping, leaning, running, twisting, and writhing during every song. The band members generally look like those of most other heavy metal bands: long, unkempt hair, loose dark shirt, leather or denim pants. The long hair is intended partly to convey a daring androgyny, partly to display a contempt for convention, but for the bass guitar player it is also a prop: Frequently he thrashes his hair in circles as he pumps away.

The crowd, avid from the start, heats up even more as the concert progresses. The pinnacle of enthusiasm is reached during the final song of the regular set. For once the lyrics of the chorus are clear because the entire crowd is singing, shouting along: "An-ti-so-cial!" It is the cry of the alienated but defiant outcast. "An-ti-so-cial!" It is a celebration of scorn,

Fans exult in the high-sensation intensity of a heavy metal concert. (Photo by Nick Romanenko)

an ecstasy of alienation. You look around at the devotees; they seem truly happy.

This closer is followed by the band's exit, then a minute or two of crowd chants and applause in an attempt to persuade them to return. Soon they do, but they do not break immediately into an encore. Instead, the lead singer leads a ritual that seems like a vulgar caricature of a religious call-and-response: "Suck my motherfucking dick!" he shouts to the crowd, and they shout it back to him. After repeating this several times, he varies the theme: "Fuck yeah!" he shouts, over and over, and again they shout it back to him each time. The crowd loves it. The usual barrier between adolescents' private profanity (with their friends) and their public restraint (with adults, especially familiar adults) is rent. Vulgarity is made public and celebrated.

After this goes on for a while, the band plays an encore and then leaves to the vigorous cheers of the crowd. During the intermission you walk around the lobby, where people are streaming toward the food/beer lines, the restrooms, the concession stands. If anything, the press of people at the concession stands is even greater than before. You wonder whether the metalheads will be able to reach the same level of intensity for the headline act, Iron Maiden.

You soon find out. Iron Maiden is greeted with even louder hosannas than Anthrax received. This band has been touring for many years, and they have developed a loyal following. You can perceive something like a melody in many of the songs Iron Maiden plays, and you can hear some of the notes of the guitar players. As for the fans, there can be little doubt of their enthusiasm. You can see easily where the term "headbanger" comes from: Many of them "bang" their heads up and down to the rhythm of the songs, eyes closed, transported. If you still cannot make out more than an occasional word of the lyrics to the songs, once again the crowd comes to your aid by singing along with many of the songs. They are especially vocal on a song toward the end of the show, an Iron Maiden classic from their early days, called "The Number of the Beast." "Six! Six! Six!" they shout together. "The number of the beast!" Looking around you, you see a young woman shouting the words, her face radiant with joy. The encore that follows is a hit from the band's latest album. "Bring your daughter, bring your daughter, to the slaugh-ter!" the crowd shouts along joyfully, "let her go, let her go, let her go!" Over and over again they sing this.

The band exits at last. The drummer throws several drum sticks to the crowd, and metalheads reach and scramble for them the way medieval peasants might have strained to grasp a reputed fragment of the cross of Jesus. At last the crowd exits, and you with them.

The concert as a manhood ritual

As bizarre as a heavy metal concert may seem to a nonfan witnessing one for the first time, it is actually not unlike other cultural rituals that have been constructed by people in other places and other times. The precise form of the spectacle may be new, but the group psychology of it, as well as the yearning for ritual and ecstatic transcendence that underlies it, are ancient and go very deep. Specifically, the heavy metal concert could be said to resemble the manhood rituals that have taken place for centuries in many cultures around the world.[2] Typically, these rituals serve the function of publicly inducting boys into the role requirements that will be expected of them as adult men. However, although the heavy metal concert contains some of the age-old elements of manhood rituals, it differs in that it leads adolescent boys *against* adult ideals; it represents a declaration of rejection of the ways of the adults in the larger culture. It is all spectacle and no sacrament; it leads not to an embrace of the moral demands of their culture but to a defiant rejection of all moral demands.[3]

Let us look around the world at what occurs to boys when they reach adolescence and at the rituals that mark male adolescence. Such a comparison highlights the ways in which the heavy metal concert is a ritual of adolescence, and also the ways it is different from traditional rituals. The comparison will also illustrate how the passage to adulthood in the contemporary United States is in some ways unusually ambiguous and problematic.

In cultures nearly everywhere there are clear expectations for what it means to be a man and clear guidelines for how to go about achieving manhood status.[4] Virtually always these expectations and guidelines are upheld and promoted by the adult men of society. From their fathers, grandfathers, uncles, and other men, boys learn what they must do, how they must behave, what they must believe, and what they must achieve in order to be considered worthy to be called a man. Almost universally the expectations are that in order to be a man, an adolescent boy must learn how to *procreate*, *provide*, and *protect*. For the requirement of learning to procreate the emphasis is on reproduction, not merely on sexuality; if boys are encouraged to experiment sexually in adolescence, it is understood that this is a way of learning how to perform adequately as a husband so that they may successfully conceive children. They must learn how to provide, too, not just for themselves but for their families; in many cases they also learn to make a contribution to the community as a whole. They also learn how to protect family and community, from animal and human predators. These three tasks must be mastered during adolescence before a boy is deemed worthy to marry and be considered an adult.

Observe the East African Samburu for illustration. Often the path to mastering these tasks begins with a formal ritual.[5] A boy's adolescence begins at age fourteen to fifteen, with a ritual of circumcision. No anesthetic is provided, yet the boy must remain utterly still during the procedure; should a boy cry out or even flinch, he will shame not only himself but his entire lineage—in the present and for generations to come. This initiation is followed by a tribal festival in which there is music, singing, costumes, and vigorous dancing. The nubile girls sing songs taunting the newly initiated young men for never having been on a cattle raid; men often conduct such raids against neighboring tribes, but the boys have not yet taken part. For the boys, the combination of music and sexual provocation reaches such a height of intense sensation that the characteristic response is "shivering," a shaking and palpitating movement of their entire bodies. Thus inspired, the boys soon go forth on their first cattle raid.

Over the next twelve years the cohort of boys who have been circumcised together learns together how to procreate, provide, and protect, instructed in all of these tasks by elders. They have sexual involvements with various girls, they learn to steal cattle and to tend the ones they steal, and they learn to protect their tribe from the depredations of other tribes. In all of this the boys are encouraged, instructed, and admonished by the adult men of the tribe. In this way the continuity of generations is maintained, and the skills and knowledge necessary for survival are passed on.

Almost always performing the tasks of manhood requires taking risks of one kind or another. Courting young women and having intercourse carry the risks of rejection and of revealing ignorance or impotence during intercourse. Learning to provide often carries physical risks; the Samburu boys must steal cattle from other tribes, and so they risk being caught and imprisoned or beaten or worse. The task of protection carries the obvious risks involved in warfare, of being injured or killed by enemies. Cultures have ways of coaxing or coercing the more reticent or timid boys—among the Samburu, no one may resist the ritual of circumcision—but for the most part boys do not need to be coaxed or coerced. Cultures simply make use of the heightened appetite for strong sensation, for intense experience, that occurs as part of adolescent development.[6] This heightened sensation seeking means that most adolescent boys find taking risks exciting, thrilling. The pleasure of the intensity of the experience may overwhelm any fears they might have that the risk might end badly for them.

One function of the intensified socialization of adolescent boys that occurs in manhood rituals is to take their thirst for high sensation and temper it, mold it, shape it so that it is not disruptive to the community but is actually useful to it. The Samburu thus socialize sensation-seeking desires so that they are in the service of the needs of the community to provide for and protect its members. William James, writing a century ago,[7] commented on some of the favorable aspects of war—that young men are often selfless, courageous, and loyal to one another during wartime in ways that they would not have been off the battlefield. He concluded that what the world needs is the *moral equivalent of war*—some strenuous and challenging activity for young men that engages all their faculties the way war does and inspires them to direct their energies on behalf of collective ideals the way war does—but does not involve killing and destruction. This insight was penetrating but incomplete. What appeals to young men about war is not only the moral quality of it but the sensory intensity of it. To fire their excitement and imaginations the way war does would require not the moral but the sensory equivalent of war. Manhood rituals around the world serve a function of this kind, providing adolescent boys with high sensation in a way that is controlled by adults and made to be in service to the community. A heavy metal concert is also, in a way, the sensory equivalent of war—but without the guiding, socializing influence of adults to make it socially constructive.

Ritual and contemporary adolescents

Looking at the American majority culture[8] in contrast to cultures such as the Samburu, it is evident how little American adults provide children in the way of ritual[9] or in the way of formal guidance and instruction for adult life. There is no recognition of the entrance to adolescence—girls, of course, have the common biological marker of menstruation, but boys in the American majority culture have nothing at all. The guidelines for procreating, providing, and protecting are poorly defined. Sexual activity in adolescence takes place with no sense of how it is connected to preparation for marriage and procreation; often it is simply recreational. There is no community of adults who instruct boys in how to provide for their future families. What instruction does take place is conducted by teachers who are strangers or near-strangers to the boys' parents and with whom boys are familiar for a year or so before moving on to the next. As for protection, learning to protect home and community from animals is hardly necessary in a modern industrialized society. Threats from human attackers (that is, violent criminals) are a problem in some parts of the United States, but nothing that most boys learn from adult men prepares them to protect their future families from such attackers.[10]

Thus adolescent boys growing up in the contemporary American majority culture are left to construct their development on their own to a remarkable extent. We allow this partly because we can afford to. Unlike most societies of the past and many societies of the present, the majority of members of contemporary Western societies have little to worry about, whether in the way of procreating enough children to sustain the next generation, providing enough food to stave off starvation and extinction, or protecting themselves from aggressive neighboring groups who are trying to steal from them, kill them, or both.[11] Because of this, it would not make sense for Americans to emulate the rituals of a culture like the Samburu, who bring their boys into adulthood so strictly and carefully because their dangerous environment requires boys to be well-prepared at an early age to meet its challenges. We can afford to relax the reins of socialization and leave our adolescents free to experience the exhilarating—if also somewhat disconcerting—air of freedom.

Left to themselves, however, some adolescent boys will follow the lure of their sensation-seeking impulses in ways that are disruptive to social order and, ultimately, to themselves. Consider two of the most prominent problems of contemporary American society: automobile fatalities and crime. Young males dominate the statistics of both. As is well known, automobile accidents are the leading cause of death among young people aged 15–24,[12] and males in this age group have the highest rate of automobile injuries and fatalities among the entire population.[13] This is not simply a result of inexperience—they drive faster, are more likely to drive while intoxicated, and take more risks while driving.[14] Adolescent boys also dominate the statistics on criminal activity.[15] Remove adolescent boys from the crime statistics of contemporary America, and the rates of a wide variety of crimes plummet. In both automobile accidents and crime, sensation seeking plays a key role[16]—adolescents drive recklessly and commit crimes in greater proportion than the rest of the population at least partly because they find these activities *exciting* and *fun*. Adolescents are high in sensation seeking, and these activities are high in sensation.[17]

This suggests that most cultures have an intensive period of socialization for adolescent boys, not just to teach them the practical ways of survival in their culture but to stamp indelibly on their hearts and souls the impulse control, the capacity for self-restraint and self-denial, the moral demands, that adolescent boys must learn if a culture is to avoid being disrupted by the sorts of things that adolescents boys may do if left on their own, unsocialized. This intensified socialization becomes crucial at puberty, when the sensation-seeking tendency reaches its peak[18] and when the physical size and strength of boys lurches upward, so that it is no longer possible to ensure their compliance with social norms merely through the greater size and strength presented by adult men. As a consequence, many cultures seize this moment in development to intensify socialization so that the control of adolescent boys becomes their own self-regulation, part of themselves. *Self-regulation* includes the capacity to control one's behavior so that it complies with social norms as well as the capacity to control one's emotions so that they do not become overwhelming; it is a crucial part of socialization. Once self-regulation is internalized, it is not necessary to impose external controls upon them as an alien and oppressive force.

Recall the Samburu. Requiring absolute stillness while the tender, acutely sensitive foreskin of the penis is sliced away during circumcision is a way of demonstrating, unequivocally, the power of the community over the individual. You must, you will, conform to the exacting requirements of self-denial and obedience, or suffer a social exile far more painful and enduring than the physical procedure of circumcision. Yet the very intensity of the procedure, and all the ritual that surrounds it, infuses it with a meaning that makes the adolescent boy's self-control at this moment seem like an achievement on his part, not merely his acquiescence to the superior power of the group. He has learned about it long before, he knows that adults place a supreme importance on it, and now his participation makes it his own, makes self-regulation part of his own identity.

A heavy metal concert can be seen as a substitute manhood ritual, a ritual that developed in part to fill the social vacuum left by a culture that disdains rituals. As in other manhood rituals, adolescent boys at a heavy metal concert are gathered together in one place and bound together by a common enthusiasm. As in other manhood rituals, high sensation is central and is delivered in part through the use of music. As in other manhood rituals, the response to this high sensation is active, visceral: The Samburu shiver, the metalheads bang their heads. As in other manhood rituals, adolescent boys at a heavy metal concert subject themselves to an imposing physical test—in the case of the heavy metal concert, the test is to withstand the immense volume of the music as well as the battering of bodies in the slamdancing pit—and are challenged not just to endure it but to glory in it.

The crucial difference between a heavy metal concert and other manhood rituals, of course, is that unlike other such rituals a heavy metal concert is not administered and overseen by adults who represent what the culture as a whole wants adolescent boys to become. It is safe to say that most American parents would not relish the prospect of their boys converting to the alienated view of life exemplified by heavy metal performers. And yet, left on their own without instruction and social pressure from significant adults, this is the ideal that many adolescent boys have chosen to celebrate and pursue. American adults encourage their children toward independence, self-sufficiency, and individualism from an early age, believing that these are healthy goals for development. What is unintended, unanticipated, and often unrecognized is that, for some adolescents, independence easily becomes loneliness, self-sufficiency may shade into isolation, individualism may take an alienated form.

The alienated individualism of American adolescents, as displayed in the heavy metal subculture, is the focus of this book. By "alienation" I mean a sense of estrangement from one's culture, a deep loneliness arising from a lack of gratifying emotional connections to others, and cynicism about the ideals and possibilities for life offered by one's culture. I see heavy metal as a response to a crisis of meaning in the lives of adolescents. My argument is that alienation is pervasive among American adolescents, including many who are not heavy metal fans, and that it is displayed with unsettling clarity in the heavy metal subculture and the lives of the metalheads.

Heavy metal is a reflection of the alienation that many adolescents feel as a result of the lack of instruction provided to them by their culture, including family, school, community, and religion. It reflects, furthermore, a failure to provide them with sufficient instruction in what should be valued and what rejected, what is good and what is evil, and what they should do with their lives. This portends, if not cultural death of the kind Philip Rieff warns about in the epigraph that opens this chapter, then at least a serious cultural problem. The music and subculture of heavy metal are symptoms of a pervasive failure of socialization in American society. The American majority culture is failing to bring a substantial proportion of its children and adolescents to adulthood with a secure sense of cultural membership; in fact, many young people stand on the threshold of adulthood deeply suspicious of the adult world they are about to enter, contemptuous of many of the institutions adults would have them embrace. From the mouths of metalheads comes a cry of alienation that speaks volumes not just about heavy metal music, but about what it is like to be an adolescent growing up in contemporary Western society.

PROFILE

Nick

Nick was known to his friends as "Rooster." With his frizzy red hair extending in every direction from his head, it was easy to see why. He wore a knit yellow shirt and nice blue jeans over his muscular frame. He had a somewhat hard face, even when he smiled, but he was garrulous and open in the interview. He was also generous: Unsolicited, he loaned dozens of tapes to me during the course of the study, so that I could get a sense of different groups and different subtypes of heavy metal.

Nick especially liked heavy metal songs with serious social commentary. Favorite songs he named included one by Slayer "about how terrible the Nazis were to the Jews," one by Dr. Know "about a city obliterating the Amazon rain forest," and songs by Exodus about dropping the atomic bomb and about child abuse. Like many metalheads, he also listened to heavy metal to purge his anger. "If I get in an angry or violent mood, to tell you the truth, I'll put it in and I'll turn it up. A lot of times it just reflects how I feel." The effect of it, he said, is that "it calms me down." Slamdancing at concerts served the same cathartic function for him: "Any angry aggressions you have, you just let them out."

This was the characteristic response of boys in the study: Most commonly, heavy metal songs served the function of helping to purge their destructive and self-destructive urges. For Nick, however, there was one occasion when listening to a heavy metal song fortified his resolve to feign a suicide attempt. He had joined the Marine Corps in the expectation of becoming an officer and a helicopter pilot. However, during boot camp marijuana was discovered in his blood, evidently the residue of smoking the drug just before he entered service. His chance to become an officer was ruined with this, yet he was contractually committed to completing his hitch. Desperate and miserable, he decided to cut his wrists in the hopes of getting a discharge for psychological reasons. And he put on a song from a heavy metal tape for background.

It's a real pretty song and a real depressing song, a slow ballad. [Is it by a heavy metal band?] Yeah. It's about a guy that wants to be taken away. "Beautiful dream, take me away, take me away from here." I guess I never really even thought about it till right now, but that was an appropriate song. It was a song I really liked and probably the only song I could have done anything to. And if I hadn't done it then, I probably wouldn't have been able to do it. So I put that on, and I cut my wrists, and they sent me to the hospital. I didn't do it to commit suicide, I just did it because I didn't know how else to get out of there.

Nick's childhood family life was chaotic and full of conflict. His mother was an alcoholic, his father physically abused him, and his parents were divorced when he was five.

[My father] used to beat me and my mom when I was little, and that's the reason for the divorce. After the divorce, he beat me up whenever I would come to visit. And then when I came to visit when I was about seventeen or eighteen, I picked him up and body-slammed him on the cement, and he hit his head. Since then he's talked stern with me, but he hasn't hit me.

Now that his father had remarried, there was resentment on Nick's part toward his father's new family, even though Nick saw them only occasionally. There was also a great deal of anger remaining toward his father, increased now by Nick's perception that his father favored the stepson. His father was putting the stepson through college but had refused to support Nick financially to attend art school, which left Nick seething. "It's something I don't think I can ever forgive him, regardless if he gives me a hundred thousand dollars, a million dollars, I'd still have that resentment toward him."

At the time of the interview Nick was employed using his artistic abilities, drawing graphic art for an automobile parts company. However, he had hopes of owning his own business doing artwork for heavy metal bands and other pop music performers. Within ten years, he said, "I'd like to own my own art studio and make a successful living at that. Do work for rock groups and get to know them, become their friend. Like Andy Warhol did." But this was just one of the possible futures he imagined for himself.

I could own a different kind of business. One might be a pawn shop, 'cause you can get fantastic bargains if people don't come back and get their stuff. And I've worked for one part-time and I know what goes on, and I've pawned stuff. The other two businesses I might like to own go together, and ironically they're a bar and a liquor store. [Why is that ironic?] Because I don't advocate drinking, you know. But I figure it would always be good business.

There is, of course, an additional irony in the son of an alcoholic mother wanting to own a bar and a liquor store.

Nick seemed bright, talented, and energetic. Perhaps he would succeed in one or more of the goals he had in mind. But there was also the danger that his propensity for recklessness would lead him to a much different fate. His stories of reckless driving were especially disturbing. The sensation-seeking thrill of driving at high speeds was compelling to him—"going fast, it stimulates you," he said—and he did not appear to worry much about the potential consequences. He had an exaggerated confidence in his ability to escape the consequences of driving recklessly, a sense of invulnerability that made him dismiss the dangers his driving practices held for him and others.

I do a hundred and ten in a Cavalier. I've blown tires at high speeds. I've done things in cars by myself when nobody else was around, just to know that I could do it. Yeah, I drive reckless in some cases, but I would not endanger other people's lives. To other people, yes, it may seem like I am, and to some degree I am, but so is everybody every time they get in a car. The one thing I have going for me in any situation is not to panic.

He also recounted, during the interview, several episodes of drunk driving and three occasions of being threatened with a gun (by three different people). He may yet face a situation where "not panicking" is not enough.

Summary profile: Nick

Age: 23
Race: White

Education: high school graduate
Current occupation: graphic artist/darkroom technician
Father's occupation: record company distribution manager
Mother's occupation: homemaker
Family background: Parents divorced when he was five, mother alcoholic, father
    physically abusive
Spent most of childhood in: Chicago and Wisconsin
Number of heavy metal recordings owned: over 200
Favorite heavy metal groups: Dr. Know, Exodus, Slayer
Goals in ten years: own a business (art studio, pawn shop, bar)
Political orientation: "inactive" Republican
Religious orientation: agnostic
Hobbies/leisure preferences: plays some bass guitar
Three people most admired: David Lee Roth, Andy Warhol, Mark Twain
Number of times in past year:

Driven a car under the influence of alcohol:	2–5
Driven a car over 80 miles per hour:	11–20
Driven a car greater than 20 mph over speed limit:	21–50
Had sex without contraception:	0
Had sex with someone not known well:	0
Used marijuana:	0
Used cocaine:	1
Used illegal drugs other than marijuana or cocaine:	0
Damaged or destroyed public or private property:	0
Shoplifted:	0

2

Heavy Metal Music and
the Socialization of Adolescents

It is individualism, and not equality, that has marched inexorably through our history. . . . [In the present] this individualism may have grown cancerous.

—**Robert Bellah et al.,** *Habits of the Heart*

This is a book about adolescence in contemporary America, using heavy metal music and its appeal for many adolescents as a framework for discussion. I am not suggesting that all adolescents like heavy metal music, and I do not contend that all metalheads are alike. However, I do contend that certain characteristics that are common among the metalheads are true of enough American adolescents to merit the attention and concern of the rest of us. Principal among these characteristics are alienation, cynicism, and a radical individualism that leaves adolescents with only the scarcest of ties to family, community, and the larger society.

These characteristics are more likely to be true of metalheads than of other adolescents, and we should be wary of generalizing too readily from metalheads to all adolescents. However, it could be argued that the metalheads display, in bold relief, characteristics that are true to some extent for many if not most American adolescents. It should also be recognized that the following for heavy metal music consists not merely of a few thousand aberrant adolescents but many millions of American adolescents in every city and town of this country (as well as adolescents in other countries around the world). The top heavy metal bands routinely sell millions of copies of every album they release and play on concert tours to packed arenas all over the United States. The popularity of heavy metal has grown, too, in the past decade. When MTV began in 1981, it avoided or ignored heavy metal bands. Now heavy metal videos appear routinely on the music video channel, and the regular segments devoted entirely to heavy metal videos are among the most popular programs on the channel. "Beavis and Butthead," a cartoon program on MTV depicting the adventures of two metalheads, has become immensely popular and is shown daily on the network. If popular culture reflects society, does all this mean that the alienation and cynicism expressed in heavy metal songs is growing among American adolescents?

Qualities like alienation are difficult to measure even in the present, much less retrospectively and historically. Nevertheless, looking at trends among American adolescents over the half century since World War II, it is difficult to avoid the conclusion that something disturbing has taken place during this time. Whether one looks at rates of suicide, crime, drug use, or automobile fatalities, a pattern of disintegration is evident. The rate of suicide among adolescents increased over 300 percent between 1950 and the late 1970s[1] and has remained high since then. This increase occurred primarily among white adolescent boys—the group most attracted to heavy metal music. The rise in crime among adolescents has been stunning. In 1950 the arrest rate for persons aged 14–24 was under 10 per 1,000 persons; by 1985 it had risen to over 100 per 1,000 persons.[2] Statistics on illegal drug use do not go back that far—perhaps because use of illegal drugs was so rare at midcentury that it did not occur to anyone to record a statistic for it—but arrests for drug use among 18- to 24-year-olds were more than 10 times higher in 1985 than in 1965.[3] The rate of automobile fatalities among adolescents aged 15–24 rose by over 50 percent between 1940 and 1980—a time when rates were actually declining in most other age groups.[4]

The recitation of these grim statistics is not meant to imply that all contemporary adolescents are headed toward self-destruction, nor is it meant to imply that heavy metal music or popular culture in general is somehow responsible for it all. It is, however, meant to raise the questions: What sort of changes have taken place in American society that have contributed to the increase in these problems? What is it about the way we socialize children and adolescents that makes it possible for these problems to occur at the rates that they do?

This is a book, then, not only about adolescent fans of heavy metal music but about the *socialization* of adolescents in the contemporary United States. Socialization is the process by which people learn the ways of the social world—the culture—in which they live. The increases in adolescents' reckless and self-destructive behavior described above, as well as the appeal of heavy metal music, can be explained partly by reference to this process. It is the central contention of this book that some adolescents are attracted to heavy metal music because of what their socialization has failed to provide for them, that is, because it has failed to teach them adequately how to function in the world. In their search for alternative sources of instruction, some of them use heavy metal songs and spectacle as one such source.

I can explain this contention by describing in more detail what the socialization process involves. Socialization typically has three goals: (1) to establish the internalization of impulse control, the development of self-regulation; (2) to prepare children and adolescents for adult social roles, including an occupational role, the role of spouse, and the role of parent; and (3) to teach sources of meaning, in other words to teach what is important, what is to be valued, what is to be lived for.

Heavy metal music is importantly related to all three of these goals. It works against the goal of establishing self-regulation, because it exemplifies and glorifies the unrestrained expression of sexual and aggressive impulses. At the same time, perhaps paradoxically, it makes it easier for adolescent fans to control their aggressive impulses because the music often has the effect of purging their anger, calming them down. Heavy metal also provides a focus for the goal of learning an occupational role for those boys who hope and plan to be involved in heavy metal music either as performers or in some other way that connects them to it. But it is to the third goal, teaching sources of meaning, that heavy metal music is most relevant. Many metalheads find a crucial source of meaning in their involvement with heavy metal, not just from the way they resonate to the lyrics of the songs but from their admiration of the performers, from their participation in the collective ritual of the heavy metal concert, and from becoming part of a youth subculture that shares not merely music but a way of looking at the world.

It may seem strange that adolescents would look to something like heavy metal music as a source of meaning, and it *is* strange, it is a reflection of the uniqueness of our time. Perhaps the most explicit and obvious source of meaning in most cultures is religious beliefs; in virtually every culture throughout human history religious beliefs have been developed to explain the origin of human life, the reasons for human suffering, and the destination of the soul after death. But most cultures have many other sources of meaning: family relationships, attachments to community or ethnic group or racial group or nation, status in a group hierarchy, accumulation of wealth, and other sources. That heavy metal could also be one such source demonstrates that the human propensity for finding sources of meaning is highly flexible and that there is tremendous variability in the sorts of experiences and ideas and symbols that may serve this yearning.

It also demonstrates, I think, that the sources of meaning common to other cultures and other times have become diluted or have dried up altogether in the American majority culture in our time. In particular religion, family, and community have all declined as sources of meaning in the last half century, as I will describe in detail in the chapters to come. At the same time, a new source of meaning has arisen: National and international electronic media have been developing, which tie individuals nationwide and worldwide into one culture (at least on a superficial level)[5] and which provide for some a source of meaning where other sources have proven insufficient. Heavy metal music is part of these new media.

One consequence of these changes—the decline of religion, family, and community as socialization influences, as well as the rise of electronic media—is that this is a very unusual time and place to be an adolescent. Throughout the book I will stress this point and illustrate it by providing examples from other cultures and other times. The examples are intended to illustrate, by contrast, how unusual (and precarious) it is to be growing up in the contemporary American majority culture.

Socialization, broad and narrow

In this chapter I present a theory of socialization that will serve as the framework for our discussion of issues concerning heavy metal music and adolescent socialization throughout the rest of the book.[6] This theory distinguishes between two general patterns of socialization. Under *broad socialization,* individualism, independence, and self-expression are encouraged, with the result that a *broad* range of individual differences in abilities and desires is expressed. Under *narrow socialization,* in contrast, there are greater pressures toward obedience and conformity of thought and behavior to a culturally prescribed standard, with the result that a relatively *narrow* range of individual differences is expressed.

Socialization in the contemporary American majority culture is broad and especially exalts the broad socialization value of *individualism.* Americans value independence, autonomy, and self-sufficiency and teach these values in direct and indirect ways to their children. This is a paradoxical form of socialization. Socialization entails the shaping of the behavior, attitudes, and worldviews of individuals so that they become what society wants them to become and conform to what society needs and expects of them.[7] In the American majority culture, however, conforming to the expectations of others is often portrayed as a weakness, a failure of character, or an unhealthy course of development.[8] Americans admire people who defy social expectations and social demands, who express their individuality to the fullest and seem not to care what others think. This is an American ideal personified by characters as diverse as the Wild West cowboy, James Dean, and Madonna. Heavy metal fans share this American ideal. They see heavy metal performers as representations of it, and they express great admiration for them.

In most cultures socialization takes place from seven sources: family, peers/friends, school, neighborhood/community, the media, the legal system, and the cultural belief system. The family is of primary importance in socialization in every culture, but the other sources must be considered as well. Below, the characteristics of each of the sources of socialization are described in their broad and narrow forms, with a focus on socialization in adolescence. This discussion will serve as an overview of the topics to be considered in the chapters that follow, where the alienation of metalheads will be explored in relation to their socialization.

Family

In cultures with narrow socialization, parents treat their adolescents very differently than most American parents do. In India, for example, the father has unambiguous authority over his children throughout his life, not just when they are young but when they are grown as well.[9] His sons owe him respect and deference, not just as boys but into manhood. In most cases sons continue to live with their parents after they marry (a common pattern worldwide), bringing their wives home to live and raising children with the assistance and instruction (not always welcome) of their parents. In this way a hierarchy of authority according to age is maintained throughout the lifespan. Although a person's status certainly rises upon reaching adulthood, parents remain figures of respect and authority.

Under broad socialization, in contrast, families are much more egalitarian. This is true of most families in the American majority culture, including the families of the boys described in later chapters. Beatrice Whiting and Carolyn Edwards (1988), in their cross-cultural study of childhood socialization, observe that even before adolescence, American children are treated by their parents "as if they were their status equals. Such treatment would be inconceivable in [most other cultures], where people's relative ages are associated with their authority and right to dominate" (p. 116). The broad socialization of American adolescents is also reflected in the fact that they are given a great deal of autonomy from the family and encouraged to be independent and to strive for self-sufficiency. Adolescents spend little of their time with their parents, instead spending their time (outside of school) either in paid employment or in leisure with friends.[10]

The egalitarianism of American families and the independence of adolescents in relation to their families emerge in some interesting ways in the lives of the metalheads. This approach to socialization leaves parents in a tenuous position when their adolescent boy brings home a tape called *Kill 'Em All* or shows an enthusiasm for a group called Slayer or Rigor Mortis. Some parents consider it to be a matter of their adolescents' free choice and do not consider themselves to have a right to object. Other parents are concerned about the potential effects of the music, but broad socialization, with its emphasis on independence and equality, gives them little ground on which to object. We will explore these issues in more detail in Chapter 6.

Peers/friends

Perhaps because they spend so much time with them at school, friends are often highly significant figures in lives of adolescents, more than in cultures where children stop going to school before adolescence. We will see in Chapter 7 that for many metalheads their friends are the most reliable and important emotional figures in their lives. This emotional tie makes peers significant as socializers, too. If one of the goals of socialization is to establish the internalization of impulse control (as part of self-regulation), peers can be an *anti*socialization influence, in that they may encourage one another to follow their impulses and violate the norms and rules of society. A heavy metal concert of the kind described in Chapter 1 is in one sense a collective celebration of their resistance to attempts by family, school, the legal system, and religion to circumscribe their behavior, to tell them what they may do and what they may not do. However, peers are not an antisocialization influence in all cultures. In cultures with narrow socialization, peers tend to promote the same norms and rules as adults.[11]

Even in a culture with broad socialization, such as the American majority culture, peers almost always expect conformity to one another within the peer group. As we will see in Chapter 4, metalheads are often highly conscious of who is a true metalhead and who is a "poseur," a phony who pretends to be a metal devotee but is not a true believer. They apply this distinction to heavy metal fans as well as to performers and base it partly on conformity to the metalhead style of dress as well as on shared belief in the metalhead ideology of alienated individualism. Metalheads, like others, tend to prefer as friends people who are similar to themselves in various ways, a process known as *selective association*. In Chapter 4 we will see how the similarities that are often the basis for friendships among metalheads include not only their common enthusiasm for heavy metal music, but also their goals for their lives and their high sensation-seeking personalities.

Schools

If you were to visit a typical American high school, you would be likely to see some students wearing black t-shirts with the logo of a heavy metal band. During classes you would find students working independently most of the time. During breaks in classes and at lunch you might see students gathering in small groups outdoors, listening to music on a portable tape player someone has brought along or listening to their own miniature tape players with headphones. Some of these groups are shrouded in cigarette smoke. These kinds of behavior are a reflection of the relative leniency of American schools and the broad socialization approach that allows a wide arena for self-expression. This is in sharp contrast to the narrow socialization of schools in Japan, for example, where children wear uniforms, do most of their work in teacher-led groups, and are responsible for serving and cleaning up at lunch.[12]

American schools strongly promote students' self-expression and self-esteem and impose few demands for conformity and obedience. The recent trend in American education, in fact, is to make classroom learning entirely individualistic, so that the teacher does very little teaching of the class as a whole and instead attempts to tailor the curriculum individually for each child.[13] However, the result of this individualistic approach to education is often not creativity and engagement but boredom and loneliness, as we shall see in more detail in Chapter 7.

Community

Until recently in human history (and even now for much of the world) most people grew up in a small community and lived there all their lives. Each person would have many members of the family and extended family living in the same household or nearby and would also be familiar with many if not all of the other members of the community. Families typically had roots in the community extending back many generations. This was a social environment highly conducive to narrow socialization, for better and for worse. For better, each child would grow up with the security of having many people around who knew him well and were concerned with his well-being. For worse, the press toward conformity in such a community would be intense, and anyone who resisted would risk social isolation. The most sensitive and creative souls would be likely to suffer most.[14]

What happens when the characteristic form of the community changes and becomes larger, more diverse, more permeable as people become free to move out or move in? We are in the process of finding out. The past 300 years have witnessed a steady and steep decrease in the proportion of communities that fit the profile of the traditional community. In Western societies, by now, most cities are too large for people to know most of the other people who live there. The membership of the community is constantly in flux as families move in or out following the parents' occupational paths from one part of the country (or the world) to another. Extended families living in the same community are increasingly rare, and extended families sharing a household are extremely rare. In Chapter 6 I will offer some examples that indicate how this lack of community cohesion contributes to adolescent alienation.

The heavy metal subculture provides a partial substitute for this absence of community. Most metalheads proclaim a certain sense of connection with other metalheads based on their shared enthusiasm for the music. This shared enthusiasm can also be the basis of establishing new friendships for a metalhead who moves into a new school or a new community. The analogy should not be carried too far, however. Being part of a community of metalheads bears only the weakest resemblance to being part of a geographically distinct traditional community. A traditional community has authority over its members, authority to reward, coerce, and punish. The ties that exist between individuals in a traditional community are stable and usually lifelong. In comparison, ties based on liking heavy metal music are superficial and transient, easily dissolved, and the authority that metalheads have over one another is limited to acceptance as an authentic metalhead or rejection as a fake, a poseur.

Media

Cultures vary in the range of media they allow their members to have access to. In cultures with narrow socialization, the range is narrow, and the content of media is controlled by government authorities (North Korea and Iran are contemporary examples). In the United States and other Western societies the range of media offerings is broad, reflecting the broad socialization that predominates there. There is a remarkable diversity of media in these societies. The implication for socialization is that to a large extent individuals in these cultures may choose from this buffet of media choices the ones that most appeal to them and are most consistent with their particular desires and inclinations. This is a kind of *self-socialization*, in which individuals are free to choose the materials that contribute to their socialization.[15]

Heavy metal music is one of the media options available to adolescents, and it is one of the materials some of them use toward their socialization. As noted above it is relevant to all three goals of socialization: impulse control, preparation for adult roles, and finding sources of meaning. It legitimizes their resistance to demands for impulse control; however, as we shall see in Chapter 5, it also makes it easier for them to control their aggressive impulses, because for many of them it has the effect of calming them down when they are angry. It provides a potential (and highly idealized) occupational path for boys (and some girls) who envision themselves as future heavy metal stars or as involved in the business end of heavy metal. (Their heavy metal dreams will also be described in Chapter 5.) And it provides a crucial source of meaning for many of them, helping them to make sense of the world around them or at least giving them the comfort of knowing that they are not the only ones who have decided that it makes no sense.

Legal system

The legal system is part of socialization in the sense that it sets certain limits to behavior and in doing so demands a degree of impulse control. Although the legal system is not an important part of childhood socialization, in adolescence and beyond it may play an important role by demarcating the range of acceptable behavior and establishing the severity of punishment for deviating from that range.

The controversy over whether to place legal restrictions on the distribution of heavy metal music is, in part, a debate about socialization, about how much adolescents' desires and behavior should be restricted. Few critics of the music have suggested banning it outright. Rather, their argument has been that the sale of some of the recordings should be restricted to people who are above a certain age. The narrow socialization argument is that society has a responsibility to restrict children's access to materials that may be harmful to their moral and social development. People making this argument would say that many of the songs described in Chapter 3 are potentially harmful to young people because they contain themes of violence, hatred, and despair. According to this view, then, the legal system should put appropriate limits on the materials children and adolescents may buy and prohibit them from purchasing potentially harmful materials when they are away from the eyes of their parents. The broad socialization argument is that adolescents have a right to listen to any music they choose, no matter what adults might think of it. With the First Amendment guarantee of freedom of speech, the American legal system declares itself generally in favor of broad socialization in this respect.

Although socialization is generally broad in European countries, socialization in the legal system in European countries is substantially narrower than in the United States with regard to issues of freedom of speech and freedom of the press. Recently in Europe a youth subculture of neo-fascist skinheads has developed, composed mostly of adolescent boys and young men. One of the unifying trademarks of this subculture is their music, known as "Oi" music. It is characterized by punk-style music and lyrics that hurl insults and threats to foreign "guest workers" and immigrants. Sales of Oi music have increased steeply in recent years, with hundreds of thousands of units sold annually across Europe.

The government of Germany has had no qualms about banning Oi music. This reflects narrower socialization in the legal system; specifically, it is an attempt to narrow the range of influences to which people are exposed if the effect of such influences may be to incite hatred and social conflict. In the United States, similar attempts to suppress "hate speech" and related media have met with greater obstacles in the legal system. The American legal system is inclined toward broader socialization; in the trade-off between freedom of expression and maintaining social order, the American tendency is to accept a certain amount of social disorder in order to maintain the principle of free speech, whereas to Europeans the ideal of freedom of speech is less sacred, and they are willing to accept certain limits on free speech in an effort to promote social stability.

Cultural belief system

The cultural belief system is the system of norms and moral standards of a society, the ideals and values that set expectations for behavior. The cultural belief system is not only a source of socialization in its own right, but also one that provides the ideological basis for socialization from the other sources.

For an example of how this works in a culture characterized by narrow socialization, consider Morocco.[16] In that northwest African country the cultural belief system is based in the religion of Islam. As in other belief systems characterized by narrow socialization, the cultural belief system of Islam promotes values such as self-restraint, interdependence, obedience to (God's) authority, and conformity to a particular way of thinking and behaving.[17] With regard to the family, Islamic teachings include the belief that the authority of the parents, particularly the father, is paramount and is not to be contradicted. Interdependence is valued over independence in the values Moroccan parents teach their children, reflecting the Islamic emphasis on consideration for others and limiting the desires of the self. With regard to school, the public school curriculum includes instruction in Islam. The legal system is also influenced by Islamic law, particularly with regard to family-related legal issues such as marriage and divorce.

In cultures with broad socialization, such as the American majority culture, the cultural belief system is one of *individualism*, and this also has pervasive effects on the socialization that takes place from the other sources. American parents tend to allow and encourage qualities such as independence and creativity, because these are the sorts of characteristics that rate highest in a cultural belief system of individualism (and so these are the characteristics parents wish their children to have). American schools tend to promote the same qualities as American parents, for the same reasons. American communities are formed of loosely connected individuals and relatively isolated families, in part because the American ideal of individualism includes freedom from the expectations and social pressures of one's neighbors. As noted above, the freedoms granted in the American media and the American legal system are also rooted in an individualistic cultural belief system.

The belief system that underlies heavy metal songs also has its roots in American individualism. In heavy metal songs, too, the right of the individual to do whatever he or she pleases is enshrined among the highest values. Self-fulfillment and self-expression are held high whereas self-restraint and self-denial are scorned as the values of the timid, the dull, and the humorless. The heavy metal concert becomes a stage for acting out this ideology—by the fans in the audience as well as by the performers on stage. It is a spectacle of sensuality and impulse, of pure and uninhibited aggression.

The result, however, is not so much a celebration of life as a declaration of alienation and loneliness. Carried to the extreme, the individualism of heavy metal fans becomes an active rejection of all social institutions and all forms of social restraint. It also becomes a source of their alienation, because it gives them nothing stable and reliable to guide them in understanding the world and their places in it. Throughout this book we will explore the darker consequences of socializing adolescents according to a belief system in which individualism is taken to the extreme of hyperindividualism. This will be the particular focus of the final chapter.

Broad socialization and contemporary adolescents

A culture of hyperindividualism,[18] of broad socialization taken to its extreme, is the culture to which children and adolescents growing up in America today are heirs. The benefits of living in such a culture should not be underestimated. It opens up a freedom for self-development unprecedented in history. More than in any time or any culture in the past, individuals may choose and pursue the kind of life they wish to live. Barriers of class, race, ethnicity, and gender, though remaining considerable for some, are lower now in Western societies than they have been in most times and places of the past. Narrow socialization confers a sense of belonging and definite sources of meaning, but it can be stifling and rigid, discouraging individuals from attempting anything that may be met with social disapproval. With the broad socialization of the contemporary West, the full range of each individual's gifts—intellectual, organizational, performance, artistic, athletic, musical, personality—is invited expression.

The benefits of broad socialization are great, but there is an underside to it, as well. Given this freedom to pursue their own paths and develop their own gifts, some adolescents thrive, but others find themselves dizzied by the multiplicity of options, unable to find any choice worth pursuing. Given the freedom to find their own meanings and decide on their own beliefs, some adolescents seize the challenge, but others conclude that the world they have found themselves in has little meaning and that there is little or nothing in it worth believing in.

In the lives and words of the metalheads, a considerable amount of disorientation and disillusionment is evident, as the following chapters will illustrate. Some of them are the losers in a system of broad socialization, and they are seriously offtrack with their lives. Others are in fact doing reasonably well and are likely to go on to be reasonably successful members of American society in the love and work of their lives. But even for many of the boys who are doing reasonably well there is an element of confusion and anxiety in them, of alienation, over modern life. It is this alienation to which heavy metal music gives fierce and undiluted expression.

Mark

Mark was nearly twenty-one years old, but he did not seem that old, either in appearance or in how he lived. He was of normal adult size, maybe even a little heavier than average, but his face was that of a much younger boy—smooth and hairless, dotted with acne, braces on his teeth. His light brown hair was nicely styled and shoulder-length, and he wore wire-rimmed glasses.

There was also a distinct immaturity in his social life, more characteristic of an early adolescent thirteen- or fourteen-year-old than of a person his age. He said he had never had a girlfriend. "Nope. And I've never been out on a date. I do things with girls I consider friends. But I'm still a virgin and I haven't really gone on an official date." Would you like to? I asked. "Oh yeah," he said. "I'm just bashful—I guess that would be the word for it. I don't know how to approach somebody. I don't know how to talk to them. I've just been like that all my life. I see someone I'd like to talk to, and just before I get there I go—[visibly tenses his body]—and I walk away. But once I've been around somebody for some time, I start to feel more comfortable with that person, and then I start opening up and talking to them."

Not only in his relations to girls but in relation to other boys, his interests seemed characteristic of a younger person. He said he enjoyed playing "role-playing games" such as Dungeons and Dragons. "One of the games I'm really into now is Apocalypse, which is role-playing of the dark future," he said. "It's one of those odd ones where everyone runs around with high-powered automatic weapons and blows each other away. It's fun."

He saw heavy metal music as helping him to release excess energy. "I listen to heavy metal when I have a lot of pent-up energy to release," he said. "Usually I listen to it just before I go to bed. It helps me fall asleep. And I'll read to it. It gets me up in the morning, too. I don't get really physically active when I listen to it. I just sit there, and the music helps release some of the energy." Listening to heavy metal helped him purge this nervous energy. Slamdancing at concerts helped release a more aggressive form of

energy. "It gets rid of a lot of excess violent energy in a very controlled sort of manner," he said. "Everyone gets in a pit and just
starts throwing their arms and legs up."

He also used LSD to relax himself. He described LSD as "my
drug of choice. I don't like pot, I don't like alcohol. But for me,
LSD is a nice psychological release. Some people like to go out and
get drunk on weekends, I like to go out and drop acid on weekends."

All these unruly emotions in need of taming and release may
have had their source partly in a disrupted and unhappy family
life. His father was an alcoholic, his parents divorced when he was
two years old, and his mother remarried when he was ten. His relationships with both his father and stepfather were problematic.
"I don't see my real dad that often, once every two or three
months," he said. "One of the main reasons I don't like to go out
there [to visit] is because he's an alcoholic. And every time I go out
there, he just gets so drunk. It just makes me so mad sometimes.
My entire life, he's been an alcoholic. That's why my mother divorced him." He visits his father now out of a kind of grim duty,
"just to keep contact with him. Just to let him know, 'Dad, I'm still
alive. I'm doing all right.' And then he gets drunk and then I
leave. Kind of depressing. It's bothered me a lot that I've never
had an actual father."

His relationship with his stepfather was, if anything, even
worse. "Me and him are like black and white," said Mark. "We di-
ametrically disagree on everything. We sort of rub each other the
wrong way." Two years ago they had had a terrible fight.

> [What was the fight about?] *Something very stupid. I wanted to
> watch a TV program and he didn't want to watch it. And I said, "Mike,
> stop being an asshole." And he came up and slapped me. Just real hard,
> and it knocked my glasses off my face and cut me right across there.
> And I'm just like my real father. I have an absolutely bad temper that
> just [snaps his fingers] like that. And I turned around without even
> thinking and just slugged him right in the face and just jumped on his
> back and started punching him. I broke his knee, I gave him a hairline
> fracture on his skull, and I broke his nose. And he still has not forgiven
> me for that.*

For all his bashfulness, then, there was an undercurrent of sim-
mering violence running through Mark's life. His emotions were

polarized to one extreme or the other, and he recognized this himself. He admitted to a disturbing lack of self-regulation: "I'm usually an easygoing, nice, mellow kind of guy," he said. "But when [something] really, really bothers me, my temper just goes [snaps his fingers] like that, and I literally lose control. There's no in-between point."

Also reflecting this polarization of emotion, he could say this about his stepfather later in the interview, the stepfather he had assaulted.

[My mother] couldn't have got a better man than Mike. They're great for each other. [Even though you and he don't get along?] Well, he's a very wonderful man. He's very good. He just has different beliefs than I do, and that's why we clashed. He believes I should be doing one thing when I don't believe I should. But as far as being a nice person goes, and as far as being caring and loving, yeah, he's really nice.

This polarization of emotion was reflected in a peculiar way in Mark's tastes for heavy metal. He liked mainstream metal bands like Iron Maiden, but he also liked the hardest and harshest variety of heavy metal, the so-called "death metal" genre, where the songs typically describe the most brutal violence in the most gruesome detail. And he considered these songs not only angry and violent but *humorous*. Of course, his claim that he found them humorous may have been a way of underplaying his fascination with the songs. He recited the lyrics of a song by Rigor Mortis with peculiar absorption, but at the same time he seemed embarrassed to admit that he liked it.

I just bought a CD by Rigor Mortis. I can't figure out if the band takes themselves seriously or not. I certainly hope they do not. It's pretty gross. There's a song there called "Bodily Dismemberment," and I think it's kind of funny. The song starts out, "Welcome to my room, my dear, and I'll show you a good time. Too bad you didn't know my fetish is a crime. No need to worry, bitch, just lay there and relax. And as you reach your climax I'll be reaching for my ax." The whole album is like this. I think it's funny. I can't believe [they're serious]. If they take themselves seriously, I think that's rather sad.

Mark was a complex young man, childlike and yet prone to violence. Did his interest in heavy metal promote his tendency to violence? The most direct answer would be a flat no, because he stated himself that he uses it to expel excess energy, including (through slamdancing) violent energy. At the same time, however, one might also wonder if, in his assault on his stepfather, he was in some sense imagining himself as a character in one of the violent songs he liked so much, or perhaps as one of the mystical heroes of one of his role-playing games. In any case it is worth noting that although he liked the darkest and most violent form of heavy metal music, he was quite idealistic in his goals for his life.

[What do you see yourself doing in ten years?] *Getting my Ph.D. in marine biology and going to work for Greenpeace, or going into work in a marine wildlife preserve, or a place like Sea World or an aquarium. Just someplace where I could work with sea animals. I am definitely going to get a Ph.D. in marine biology. That is my life's goal. . . . I'm scared for the environment right now, that people are just like, "Oh, well, I'll be dead by the time it gets too bad." What about your children? What about* their *children?*

Summary profile: Mark

Age: 20
Race: White
Education: high school graduate
Current occupation: busboy
Father's occupation: chemical engineer
Mother's occupation: insurance claims adjuster
Family background: parents divorced when he was two years old, father is alcoholic, ambivalent relationship with stepfather
Spent most of childhood in: Atlanta
Number of heavy metal recordings owned: about 40
Favorite heavy metal groups: Iron Maiden, Stormtroopers of Death, Rigor Mortis
Goals in ten years: marine biologist, work for Greenpeace
Political orientation: liberal Democrat
Religious orientation: believes God exists, but no particular theology
Hobbies/leisure preferences: "role-playing games," for example, Dungeons and Dragons
Three people most admired: friend Eric, members of Greenpeace, Martin Luther King Jr.
Number of times in past year:

Driven a car under the influence of alcohol:	2–5
Driven a car over 80 miles per hour:	6–10

Driven a car greater than 20 mph over speed limit:	>50
Had sex without contraception:	0
Had sex with someone not known well:	0
Used marijuana:	2–5
Used cocaine:	0
Used illegal drugs other than marijuana or cocaine:	>10
Damaged or destroyed public or private property:	0
Shoplifted:	6–10

What Is This Thing
Called Heavy Metal?

Technology is ideology.

—Neil Postman, *Amusing Ourselves to Death*

*[Art involves the] imitation of an action, [which arouses] pity and fear [and
then] effects the proper purgation of these emotions. . . . But to produce this effect
by the mere spectacle, and dependent on extraneous aids, is a less artistic method.*

—Aristotle, *Poetics*

*Our whole world is living through a century of spiritual illness, which could not
but give rise to a similar ubiquitous illness in art.*

—Aleksandr Solzhenitsyn, twentieth-century Russian novelist

In order to understand metalheads and the heavy metal subculture, some familiarity with heavy metal songs is essential. In this chapter I provide a brief
history of the genre, describe typical characteristics of the songs, and present
numerous lyrical examples. Let me say from the outset, however, that to get
the full effect of heavy metal music you have to listen to it, not just read a description of it. In particular, you have to listen to it in a live setting, at its
loudest and most cacophonic, with metalheads banging their heads, pumping their fists, and slamdancing all around you. For those of you who cannot
quite imagine yourselves undertaking such an enterprise, this chapter will
at least give you a general idea of the characteristics of heavy metal songs.

Before beginning I should make it clear what kinds of songs I am defin-
ing as heavy metal, because there is much debate among metalheads as to
which songs and groups do and do not qualify. For those who define the
term strictly, heavy metal includes only bands that have a harsh, dark
sound and perform songs mainly with themes of alienation and anger.
For those who define the term more loosely, heavy metal includes not
only these bands but also bands that have a brighter, lighter sound and
whose songs concern mainly boy-girl and hedonistic themes—sex, angry
love, lost love, desired love, partying, and more sex. For the purposes of

this book, I define the term more strictly (for reasons I describe below), and bands with lighter music and lyrical themes are considered not heavy metal but hard rock.[1]

Origins

In recounting the history of heavy metal, one could begin as recently as the early 1980s or as far back as the invention of the electric guitar. It was not until the early 1980s that heavy metal became a distinctive form, clearly different from hard rock; but the line leading to that development begins with the invention of amplified musical sound, in particular the invention of the electric guitar about seventy years ago. It may be worthwhile to take a brief tour of technological developments in popular music from the invention of the electric guitar to the present. Heavy metal music is a highly technological musical form. It would not exist if the technological basis for it had not developed, so the history of heavy metal music is to a large extent a history of the applications of modern electronic technology to popular music.

The electric guitar was first invented in the 1920s. Prior to this time the sound of the guitar was relatively mild. Not much volume can be achieved by the unamplified guitar, especially when it is played in individual notes rather than chords. Pianos, trumpets, and saxophones could easily dominate the guitar when the instruments were played together. But the increase in volume and power that came with electrification virtually transformed the guitar into a new instrument. Electrification allowed the guitar to be heard above the din of the other instruments, even to dominate them as a lead instrument.

In addition, electrification made possible new sounds on the guitar, sustained and distorted sounds, which opened the way to new musical forms. First a new blues arose in the 1930s and 1940s—derived from the early blues dating from about 1912[2] but changed by the new technology—then, in the 1950s, rock and roll. As further technology developed, rock music developed along with it, taking advantage of each advance in technology. In the early 1960s came the amplified bass guitar.[3] The bass guitar is the four-string, low-pitched, rhythm-keeping guitar heard in most blues, pop, rock, and heavy metal songs. In the early 1960s technology was developed that made it possible to amplify the bass guitar sound enormously, and the result revolutionized popular music. Above all the electrified bass guitar was an advance in *power:* The bass guitar is a thumping, pounding sound, at least as it is played in rock and heavy metal. It infiltrates and vibrates the ribcage when played at top volume. It can be an awesome, dark sound, like the low growl of an enormous, menacing beast. This sound was crucial to the development of rock music in the 1960s and 1970s, and it became a fundamental part of heavy metal music as well.

The beginning of heavy metal as a genre distinct from rock music is difficult to define precisely.[4] There was a gradual progression, of sorts, from rock in the middle 1960s to so-called "acid rock" in the late 1960s, to early heavy metal in the late 1960s and early 1970s. Acid rock, played by performers such as Jimi Hendrix, was so named because it was deemed to be an auditory representation of the experience of an acid (LSD) trip, that is, a musical depiction of what it is like to experience the effects of the hallucinogenic drug LSD. Acid rock songs included the usual rock components of electric guitar, bass guitar, drums, and vocals—but with a harder, darker, more abrasive edge. Heavy metal then took these musical elements one step further, without the association with LSD experiences. Most observers agree that it arose around 1969–1972, with groups such as Led Zeppelin and Black Sabbath. The term itself was popularized in the 1968 Steppenwolf hit "Born to Be Wild," which includes the phrase "heavy metal thunder" to describe the experience of riding a car or motorcycle on the desert highways of California. By 1971 the hardest rock music was being referred to as heavy metal.[5]

The new genre was distinct from rock music not only musically but in its lyrical themes. Although heavy metal shared with rock music an antiauthority stance, the emphasis on love found in rock music—love not only of the man-woman variety but love as the answer to society's ailments—was missing from heavy metal. In its place was a fascination with evil, with the dark side of the human heart and of human experience. Why this change? Sociological and psychological explanations are possible, and I will be providing some in the course of this book, but part of the explanation may also be musical, even commercial. If most other bands were doing sex, love, peace, brotherhood, and so on, one way to be original was to turn that formula on its head and do alienation, menace, destruction, and nihilism. The creative possibilities of the new musical technologies almost invited this development. Technology is ideology, as Neil Postman has observed.[6] That pounding bass guitar could be used to create a sense of chaos and doom, that electric guitar—and the new effects gadgets being developed for it, such as fuzz boxes that could increase the distortion of the sound—could be made to screech and wail. Emphasizing these possibilities could also get you noticed as a band, because it could make you sound different, novel. Whether the bands calculated it that way or not, there was a commercial niche there waiting to be filled. Throughout the 1970s groups such as Led Zeppelin, Black Sabbath, and Judas Priest had much lucrative success as heavy metal bands.

In the 1980s and into the 1990s new heavy metal bands came along, and new technologies made the heavy metal sound still darker, fiercer, more abrasive. Iron Maiden produced songs that were often broodingly introspective as well as songs based on myths and legends. Metallica and Megadeth developed a startlingly dark and energetic sound, and they used it to convey gloomy lyrical themes of religious and political hypocrisy, alienation, and existential emptiness. Slayer gained a following with songs of chaos and violence, the lyrics almost growled or snarled rather than sung. A new term, "speed" or "thrash" metal, was coined to include the heavy metal subgenre of Metallica, Megadeth, Slayer, and other bands whose sound was distinctly more aggressive than even other heavy metal groups and whose lyrical themes were relentlessly pessimistic and angry. An even more extreme genre began to develop, called "death metal" for its almost exclusive focus on songs of violence and death. Thus heavy metal in its current incarnation includes what we might call "mainstream metal," with groups such as Iron Maiden, Judas Priest, and Ozzy Ozbourne, speed/thrash metal groups such as Metallica, Megadeth, Slayer, and Anthrax, and death metal groups such as Rigor Mortis and Post Mortem who have a small but zealous following.

Metal themes, musical and lyrical: A song analysis

What are heavy metal songs about, lyrically? What do they sound like, musically? To answer these questions in a systematic way, I analyzed 115 heavy metal songs from albums released between 1988 and 1992. I chose six heavy metal bands and analyzed all songs on two albums from each of the six bands. In selecting the six bands I chose three of the most popular mainstream metal bands (Judas Priest, Iron Maiden, and Ozzy Ozbourne) and three of the most popular speed/thrash metal bands (Metallica, Megadeth, and Slayer). I wanted to have both mainstream metal and speed/thrash metal represented in the analysis, because (as we shall see) the two strains are somewhat different lyrically and musically.[7]

There are several justifications for excluding the hard rock groups from the song analysis and from the study. First, I consider hard rock to be much different from heavy metal, musically and lyrically. Musically, although both heavy metal and hard rock songs emphasize simple chord progressions, a pounding beat, a highly distorted guitar sound, and guitar solos in most songs, it is obvious even without a song analysis that hard rock songs are much more likely to be in a major key than heavy metal songs. This reflects and emphasizes a difference in lyrical themes, with hard rock lyrics focusing on the hedonistic themes described above, whereas the lyrics of heavy metal songs are generally much more serious and pessimistic. Second, the focus of the study and of the book is on adolescent alienation, and themes suggesting alienation are prevalent in heavy metal songs but rare in hard rock songs. Third, although there are frequent debates among heavy metal fans as to which groups are "really" heavy metal, there would be little argument about any of the groups I have included here. The arguments generally center around hard rock groups such as Poison, Mötley Crüe, and Guns N' Roses, and I think this reflects the fact that their lyrics and music are different from those of groups like Metallica and Judas Priest.

Anyone performing a song analysis (or reading about one) would be well advised to keep in mind that any song is open to multiple interpretations. The analysis here is not presented as the only possible result, but simply as a useful overview of the general characteristics of the songs, as background for the chapters that follow. However, it should also be recognized that the interpretations included here are not arbitrary and that the range of interpretations is not limitless. Heavy metal fans are united into a coherent subculture precisely because they share certain interpretations of the meaning of the songs. They have in common that the songs express for them the ideology of alienation that most of them share to one degree or another.

I analyzed the songs in three ways. First and most simply, I determined whether the song was performed in a minor key, a major key, or parts of each. The minor/major distinction is crucial to the general mood conveyed by a song. Minor keys are keys of dark moods and ideas: anger, sadness, fear, anxiety, betrayal, alienation, bitterness. It is difficult to convey anything but a negative mood when using a minor key. Major keys, in contrast, usually convey brighter moods and ideas: happiness, pleasure, humor, playfulness, exuberance. The range of moods and ideas that can be depicted by major keys is wider than the range for minor keys; major keys sometimes convey sadness, poignancy, anger, wistfulness, and other darker emotions and experiences. Minor keys, however, are rarely used successfully to depict what is light and bright.

The second way I analyzed the songs was according to the specific mood of the song. This was based on the lyrics as well as on the music. I used four specific mood categories: (1) anger (including aggression and defiance); (2) sadness/hopelessness; (3) fear (a song that threatens the listener or in which the main character in the song is being menaced); and (4) positive emotion (of any kind). Usually the music reinforces the theme of the lyrics, but not always. For example, the Iron Maiden song "Can I Play with Madness?" might seem, by its title and its lyrics, to be a song about fear or anxiety. Actually, however, it is a bouncy, cheerful song because of the music, which is played in a major key with a lively beat and includes vocal harmonies—qualities unusual in a heavy metal song—and so it was rated as depicting "positive emotion." More often, however, the key choice (major/minor), musical style, and lyrical themes combine in a consistent way to deliver an integrated impression to the listener.

The third element of the analysis considers lyrical theme.[8] I devised ten categories on the basis of claims about the content of heavy metal songs made by critics and apologists, as well as on the basis of my own familiarity with heavy metal songs. Lyrical themes for a particular song sometimes applied to more than one category, so there were 161 category assignments made for the 115 songs in the analysis.[9] In looking at the results of this analysis, let's move from the specific to the general, taking first the lyrical themes of the songs, then the specific moods, then the keys.

Songs of Drug and Alcohol Use

The frequencies of lyrical themes in the various categories are shown in Table 3.1. The category in which the least number of songs were classified was the category for substance use, that is, drug and alcohol use, which applied to only one song. I included this category because heavy metal music has been accused of promoting drug and alcohol use,[10] but there was no evidence in this analysis to support that accusation. In fact, the only one of the 115 songs concerning drugs or alcohol, Ozzy Ozbourne's "Demon Alcohol," is, if anything, an *anti*-alcohol song. Here is an excerpt:

> *I'll watch you lose control*
> *Consume your very soul*
> *I'll introduce myself today*
> *I'm the demon alcohol.*

TABLE 3.1   General Characteristics of Heavy Metal Songs

Lyrical Theme		Mood (frequency)	Key (frequency)
Substance use	1	Anger 57 (50%)	Minor 96 (83%)
Hatred	13	Sadness 31 (27%)	Major 10 (9%)
Violence	40	Fear 10 (9%)	Both 9 (8%)
Angst	35	Positive 17 (15%)	
Protest	21		
Satan	8		
Myths/legends	14		
Sex	8		
Love	7		
Heavy metal life	10		

The "Demon Alcohol" in the song, speaking in the first person, is trying to lure the listener into intoxication, with the clear suggestion (and implied warning) that succumbing to this lure will lead to the listener's ruin.

Songs of Hatred and Violence

Heavy metal music has been said by its critics to be characterized by songs of hatred and violence.[11] In this analysis both appear as themes in many of the songs (hatred in thirteen songs and violence in forty). For songs of hatred, the nature of the hatred expressed differs depending on the band. The hatred in many of Slayer's songs is general, in the sense that it does not seem to be directed at anyone in particular. In songs by other bands the hatred is often what we might call a principled hatred, a hatred directed toward people who are depicted in the song as being venal or oppressive, well worthy of the hatred being directed toward them. For example, both Iron Maiden and Ozzy Ozbourne have songs directing hatred toward hypocritical religious figures, and Megadeth has a notorious song ("Hook in Mouth," highly popular among metalheads) that attacks the Parents' Music Resource Center (PMRC) for its attempts to label some popular music recordings (especially heavy metal recordings) as unsuitable for tender ears. It includes this lyric:

> You say you've got the answers, well who asked you
>   anyway?
> . . . Freedom, it means nothing to me
> As long as there's a P.M.R.C.

The lyrics imply that the hatred is in defense of freedom of expression, which makes it justified, even virtuous.

Violence was a theme in forty songs, making it the most common theme in the analysis. The music of heavy metal is inherently well suited to expressions of violence; the rough, distorted guitar sound, the rumbling bass guitar, and the pounding drums would not be effective in conveying gentleness or compassion but are exceptionally effective in portraying chaos, death, war, destruction, and other violent themes. This does not mean that all of the songs about violence celebrate or advocate violence. Most of the songs of war, for example, could be called antiwar songs. Megadeth's "Architecture of Aggression" contains this lyric:

> Great nations built from the bones of the dead
> With mud and straw, blood and sweat
> You know your worth when your enemies
> Praise your architecture of aggression.

A song by Metallica entitled "One," which several of the boys in the study cited as their favorite heavy metal song, tells in the first person the story of a man who has been permanently wounded and traumatized by war:

> *Now the world is gone I'm just one*
> *Oh God, help me hold my breath as I wish for death . . .*
> *Landmine*
> *Has taken my sight . . .*
> *Taken my arms*
> *Taken my legs*
> *Taken my soul*
> *Left me with life in hell.*

In other heavy metal songs, however, violence is depicted in quite a different manner, with something like enjoyment, even zeal. The violence is most fierce and chilling in Slayer's songs. Two of their songs in the analysis involved violence toward women, and they provide prime examples of how heavy metal music has gained a reputation in some quarters as being disturbing, even evil music. Take this lyrical excerpt from their song "Kill Again":

> *Trapped in mortal solitude*
> *Lift the gleaming blade*
> *Slice her flesh to shreds*
> *Watch the blood flow free . . .*
> *No apparent motive*
> *Just kill and kill again*
> *Survive my brutal thrashing*
> *I'll hunt you till the end.*

The music that accompanies these lyrics is every bit as violent as the lyrics themselves. Nor is Slayer the only heavy metal band in the analysis with violent songs of this kind. Judas Priest has a song called "Night Crawler":

> *Straight out of hell*
> *One of a kind*
> *Stalking his victim*
> *Don't look behind you . . .*
> *Death comes in an instant*
> *As they hoped it would*

Souls ascend to heaven
Where they feast on flesh and blood.

An Ozzy Ozbourne song called "Bloodbath in Paradise" depicts the murders committed by Charles Manson and his followers in the late 1960s:

They'll summon you
To wake from the dead as you lie bleeding
Murdered in your bed
The sweetest dreams are all in your mind
But no one wakes when Charlie creeps behind . . .
Can you hear them in the darkness
Helter skelter, spiral madness, yeah
Bloodbath in paradise.

There can be little question, then, that violence is prominent in heavy metal songs and that it is sometimes violence of the most brutal kind. Of course, it should be noted here (as we shall see in more detail in Chapter 5) that listening to violent songs does not provoke most metalheads to violence but rather has the effect of purging their anger harmlessly. Still, it cannot be ruled out that the violence of the songs acts as an inspiration to actual violence in certain individuals. Millions of young people listen to these songs, and the uses they make of them are likely to be diverse.

Suicide is another violent theme that has received much attention by critics of heavy metal, some of whom assert that some heavy metal songs encourage suicide and that performers should be held responsible. In the mid-1980s Ozzy Ozbourne's "Suicide Solution" was featured prominently in congressional hearings on whether some popular music recordings should have warning labels or "Parental Advisory" stickers.[12] For years Judas Priest was mired in a lawsuit in which the parents of a boy who attempted suicide contended that the band was to blame because of alleged subliminal messages advocating suicide in its songs, which the boy listened to often. Here only one of the 115 songs analyzed concerned suicide, a song by Megadeth called "Skin o' My Teeth":

I had wrists donning slits
Flowing constantly . . .
My blood flows through the streets
Deluge from the wounds
Empty jars of sleeping pills
On the dresser in my room.

This song is a far more explicit depiction of suicide than is found in the Ozzy Ozbourne song or the Judas Priest songs that have generated so much controversy. Yet it has not received much attention from heavy metal critics, perhaps because Megadeth is not as well known (or notorious) as Ozzy and because there has been no lawsuit involving the song (as there was for Judas Priest).

Songs of Angst and Protest

A second common theme in heavy metal songs, nearly as common as the theme of violence, was angst.[13] This category includes songs portraying loneliness, existential struggles for meaning, and mental distress and disintegration. Thirty-five of the 115 songs were classified into this category. As with violence, the nature of heavy metal *music* makes angst almost inevitable as a common lyrical theme. The sounds that define the genre of heavy metal, musically, lend themselves readily to the expression of themes of angst; the writers and performers of heavy metal exploit this musical potential, which is inevitably reflected in the lyrics as well. Some lyrical examples:

Loneliness: Megadeth's "In My Darkest Hour"

> *In my hour of need*
> *Ha, you're not there*
> *And though I reached out for you*
> *You wouldn't lend a hand . . .*
> *It feels so cold, very cold*
> *No one cares for me.*

Existential struggles: Iron Maiden's "Infinite Dreams"

> *Help me. Help me to find my true*
> *Self without seeing the future . . .*
> *There's got to be just more to it*
> *Than this*
> *Or tell me why do we exist?*

Mental distress and disintegration: Slayer's "Dead Skin Mask"

> *Dance with the dead in my dreams*
> *Listen to their hollowed screams*
> *The dead have taken my soul*
> *Temptation's lost all control . . .*
> *In the depths of a mind insane*
> *Fantasy and reality are the same.*

The third most common theme in the songs, after violence and angst, was the protest theme. This is a diverse category that includes songs attacking corruption in the institutions of politics, religion, or the legal system, songs deploring the destruction of the environment, and songs declaring a general defiance against forces that might try to restrict or repress individuals. Slayer's "Blood Red" attacks ominous political figures who are "seizing all civil liberties." Iron Maiden ridicules greedy televangelists in "Be Quick or Be Dead." Metallica rages about "Halls of justice painted green/ Money talking" in "And Justice for All." Megadeth deplores the killing of endangered species in "Countdown to Extinction." Metallica's "Eye of the Beholder" warns against unnamed enemies who seek to "Limit your imagination/ Keep you where they must."

All of the songs in this category take something that is presented by some social institution or organization as true, as real, and exposes it as being false, a lie. These songs are related to songs in the angst category described above. Like the angst songs, these songs depict a turning away from society, a profound alienation from the adult world. The difference is that in the angst songs the alienation is on a more personal level, whereas the protest songs portray alienation from social institutions (political, religious, legal, and so on) rather than from individuals. In this respect these songs are a revival of the tradition of rock protest songs from the late 1960s and early 1970s, which also deplored institutional evil and hypocrisy. There is, however, a crucial difference. Although the protest songs of the 1960s deplored the state of the world, typically they also carried the hope and promise that things could and would be different in the future, that in fact the world was on the threshold of a new, utopian era of peace, harmony, and brotherhood:

> We can change the world
> Rearrange the world.

The words of this Crosby, Stills, and Nash song from the late 1960s seem quaint next to the view of the world according to heavy metal. In heavy metal songs there is no such optimism about the bright promise of tomorrow. The world is grim and bleak, the powers-that-be are utterly corrupt—and there is no prospect that things will ever be any different.

Songs of Satan and the Supernatural

Another of the charges against heavy metal music is that it promotes satanism.[14] Of the songs considered here, eight had themes involving Satan. Six were by Slayer, two by Iron Maiden. Do these songs promote satanism in any sense, or are they simply about Satan? The songs by Iron Maiden have a mystical, mythical, storylike quality to them. Both songs appear on the Iron Maiden album *Seventh Son of a Seventh Son*, where all of the songs concern the myth described in the title, in which the seventh son born to a seventh son is invested with supernatural powers. These are evidently powers for goodness, for healing. In the song "Moonchild" Satan appears, evidently trying to convince the mother to kill her supernaturally gifted child in his cradle:

> *I am the bornless one*
> *The fallen angel watching you . . .*
> *Don't you dare try to save your son*
> *Kill him now and save the young ones*
> *Be the mother of a birth strangled babe*
> *Be the devil's own, Lucifer's my name.*

The Iron Maiden songs, then, seem to be *about* Satan rather than a glorification of Satan. The attitude expressed toward Satan is negative or ambiguous. The six songs by Slayer are of a much different order. These are the kinds of songs that have alarmed the critics of heavy metal music, songs that are violent and brutal, songs that seem to beckon the listener to evil. Here are two examples.

From "Temptation":

> *Have you ever danced with the devil*
> *Has temptation ever summoned you*
> *Ever penned your name in blood*
> *Let possession slowly swallow you.*

From "At Dawn They Sleep":

> *Bloodsucking creatures of the night . . .*
> *Lock their jaws into your veins*
> *Satanic soldiers strike their prey*
> *Leaving corpses waiting for the change.*

Do such songs promote satanism? This is difficult to say. Defenders of Slayer might reply that they, like Iron Maiden, are simply telling a story. As we will see in Chapter 7, most metalheads see the question this way. Again, however, it is important to emphasize the diversity of listeners' potential reactions to and uses of the songs. It is possible that certain metalheads may take it as something more serious than mere storybook fantasy.

Satan is not the only supernatural figure who appears in heavy metal songs. Fourteen of the songs in the analysis involved legends or myths, that is, figures with supernatural powers (other than Satan). Six of these songs were on the Iron Maiden album described above, where most of the songs concern the experiences of the legendary "Seventh Son of a Seventh Son." Four of Judas Priest's songs were in this category. This excerpt from "Painkiller" is representative:

> *Faster than a bullet*
> *Terrifying scream*
> *Enraged and full of anger*
> *He's half man and half machine . . .*
> *He is the Painkiller.*

Except for the songs by Iron Maiden, many of the mythical figures in the songs in this category have the aggressive, menacing qualities of the "Painkiller" in this song.

Songs of Sex, Love (Sort of), and the Heavy Metal Life

There are also heavy metal songs in which the themes are of the more traditional rock song variety: sex, love, and the life of a pop music star. These are not common topics in heavy metal songs—there were only eight songs on sex, seven on love, and ten on the heavy metal/pop star life out of the 115 songs in the analysis (see Table 3.1). Furthermore, these songs tend to be performed by the mainstream metal bands and not by the speed/thrash metal bands. Of the twenty-five songs in these three categories combined, only three were performed by a speed/thrash metal band. This is a reflection of mainstream metal being closer to hard rock, lyrically and musically, than speed/thrash metal is.

However, heavy metal songs on sex and love are of a different nature than rock songs on these topics. Befitting the darker, gloomier, more aggressive quality of the heavy metal genre, even heavy metal songs on sex and love are dark, gloomy, and aggressive. Of the eight songs on sex, one involves child molestation (Ozzy Ozbourne's "Mr. Tinkertrain"), one involves prostitution (Judas Priest's "Love Zone"), one involves sadomasochism (Judas Priest's "Love You to Death"), and one involves necrophilia (Slayer's "Necrophiliac"). In none of the eight songs is sex untainted by some dark emotion: fear, contempt, pain. Similarly, all six songs on love express emotions of sadness or anger.

Songs on the heavy metal life bear a stronger resemblance to rock songs, in particular to rock songs celebrating the music and life of a pop star. Most of these songs (eight of ten) were by Judas Priest in this analysis. Unlike nearly all other heavy metal songs, songs in this category are

Tattoos are common among heavy metal fans and often have the same dark themes as heavy metal songs. (Photo by Nick Romanenko)

light, frivolous, fluffy. They are also celebratory, declaring how wonderful heavy metal music is and how much fun it is to be a heavy metal star. Take the Judas Priest song "Heavy Metal":

> *When the power chords come crashing down*
> *Go tearing through my senses*
> *It's for the strong, not for the weak*

In light and dark dimension
It stimulates, regenerates
It's therapeutic feeling
It lifts our feet up off the ground
And blasts us through the ceiling
Heavy metal.

It is ironic that, as this analysis indicates, almost all heavy metal songs are pessimistic and negative, yet heavy metal songs *about* heavy metal are exuberant, almost joyful. As we shall see in Chapter 5, the explanation of this paradox is that the angry, unhappy heavy metal songs have the effect of purging angry, unhappy emotions in their metalhead listeners, "stimulating and regenerating" them in the way Judas Priest describes.

Moods and keys

Given that the most common lyrical themes in heavy metal songs are violence and angst, it will come as no surprise that the mood of heavy metal songs tends heavily in the direction of anger and sadness. Table 3.1 shows the frequencies for each of the four mood categories. In analyzing the mood of the songs, I sought to take into account both music and lyrics in order to assess the overall mood impression made by the song. Unlike the ratings of lyrical themes, for which a single song could be rated in more than one category, only one mood category was assigned to each song. As I noted above, for most songs the mood expressed by the music reinforced rather than contradicted the mood expressed in the lyrics.

Anger was the mood most commonly expressed in the songs. One-half of the 115 songs were rated as having anger as the dominant mood. Sadness was the mood found in 27 percent of the songs, making it the second most common mood. Nine percent of the songs had fear as the dominant mood. A positive emotion of any kind was characteristic of 15 percent of the songs. If you take anger, sadness, and fear together as negative emotions, then a negative emotion predominated in 85 percent of the songs, whereas a positive emotion was expressed in just 15 percent. Even the minority of songs depicting positive emotion were often "positive" in a twisted way. For example, in "Mr. Tinkertrain" Ozzy Ozbourne is expressing joy at the prospect of committing pedophilia, and in "Love You to Death" Judas Priest is cheerily describing an episode of sadomasochistic sex.

As expected the songs were generally played in a minor key (see Table 3.1). This was true of 83 percent of the songs. Nine percent of the songs were played in a major key, and 8 percent went from major to minor or vice-versa in the course of the song. The predominance of minor keys in the songs matches the predominance (85 percent) of the moods of anger, sadness, and fear. As noted earlier, minor keys are well suited to expressing such moods.

In sum, a deep sense of alienation is expressed in heavy metal songs. Lyrical themes overwhelmingly portray the world as a dangerous, corrupt, despoiled place, where no one can be trusted and where violence is a constant presence. The moods and keys of the songs reinforce the sense of alienation conveyed in the lyrics. Almost always the mood is grim— anger, sadness, or fear—and the key is minor. Although there is some variation in the characteristics of the songs, the overriding sense of alienation is present in nearly all of them.

But is it art?

Heavy metal performers like to speak of themselves as "artists," and their apologists like to defend them as such.[15] In particular, heavy metal performers, fans, and apologists defend the excesses of heavy metal, and the offenses it presents to the sensibilities of the rest of society, as being part and parcel of artistic expression. Naturally (this argument goes), "respectable" society finds heavy metal art offensive, but this is neither new nor surprising. Did not their counterparts in the late nineteenth century condemn the paintings of the Impressionists in the same tones and, in the early twentieth century, the literature of James Joyce?

Now that we have taken a look at the characteristics of heavy metal songs, let's examine briefly the qualifications of heavy metal music as art. Crucial to this evaluation, of course, is how one defines art, in general terms. Heavy metal's defenders are right that art has often violated cultural and social boundaries, extending those boundaries in new and unexpected directions. If this is the only criterion one uses to define art, then heavy metal is indeed art; so is running naked down the middle of a crowded street, which also violates established social norms in most places. In most conceptions of art, there is more to it than this.

Another criterion for art in the classical, traditional sense is that it represents certain essential truths about the human condition. The audience, witnessing these representations on stage or in song or in other forms, is edified, deepened, and (paradoxically) consoled by sharing the experience of acknowledging human suffering, limitation, vanity, and mortality. This is art, in the Aristotelian sense.[16] Perhaps surprisingly, heavy metal music qualifies as art on this criterion. As this chapter has shown, most heavy metal songs are indeed about suffering, limitation, vanity, mortality, and other tragic aspects of the human condition. And metalheads, in listening to the songs, are indeed paradoxically consoled, connected, and enlivened as a consequence, as we shall see in more detail in Chapter 5.

Perhaps the best way to characterize heavy metal music is as *vulgar art*.[17] It shares certain features with art in the classical sense—the willingness to breach social boundaries, the depiction of tragic features of the human condition—but there is nothing about it that is elevated or refined,[18] nothing of the elegant and careful arrangement of parts in relation to the whole that is also part of the definition of art in the classical tradition. On the contrary, heavy metal deliberately seeks to be uncultured, unrefined, coarse, crude, loud—in a word, vulgar. In the world of heavy metal such adjectives are not insults but praise. To performers and metalheads the vulgarity of heavy metal represents originality, energy, honesty, and integrity.[19] This same vulgarity may be seen by most of the rest of society as incoherence, indiscipline, venality, and confusion. However, according to heavy metal fans and performers, these characteristics in heavy metal songs only reflect with unflinching honesty the state of the disintegrating world around them.

And why should heavy metal music be measured against classical definitions of art in any case, when such definitions are no longer widely embraced in the postmodern world of the arts? The development of popular music toward portraying angst and nihilism only parallels similar developments in painting, sculpture, orchestral music, and other arts in the twentieth century. Ozzy Ozbourne is cultural kin to Andy Warhol and John Cage. In the late twentieth century, art is not something that elevates and edifies but a mirror of the disorder and soullessness of modern life, a gesture of despair.

Even within popular music, vulgar art did not begin with heavy metal. The rock music of the 1960s and 1970s also exalted vulgarity. But heavy metal has reformulated the audaciousness and excesses of rock for the 1980s and 1990s now that rock has become tamed and respectable. The fierce challenge to social order and authority presented by rock in the 1960s and 1970s sent the boundaries of social acceptability into a hasty retreat, and that retreat eventually extended those boundaries until rock itself was incorporated and no longer presented a threat to social order.[20] Emblematic of this, the Rolling Stones, who seemed so outrageous and offensive to respectable society in the 1960s and 1970s, who personified the sneering iconoclasm of rock, by the 1980s were touring with multinational corporations as their sponsors. They had become tame paragons of acceptable pop culture.

Heavy metal came forth in part as a response to rock's new docility. Heavy metal performers made their performances and their songs outrageous enough to violate even the new, expanded boundaries of social acceptability. Increasingly sophisticated sound technology gave them the weapons they needed to create a new sound of unprecedented fierceness to accompany their fierce, defiant, angry ideology. And the adolescents of the world listened, and responded, by the millions.

Brian

Brian was as clean-cut and wholesome-looking as you could imagine. No "metalhead" look for him; he wore a plain blue t-shirt, white shorts, and athletic shoes. He had nicely groomed black hair and distinctly rosy cheeks. He was likable and articulate, self-possessed and mature. He looked like, and was, the kind of kid who might collect baseball cards and be a member of the Spanish Club at school (see Summary Profile).

He was also a fanatical Slayer fan. Why?

I just like the music. It's so full of energy. And it's really aggressive. . . . [They write songs about] problems in the world and stuff like that. . . . I'm a musician, so naturally I listen to the music. But I also listen to the lyrics, because that's the thing about heavy metal. It exposes a lot of problems. It tells the truth about what's really going on in the world, not just a bunch of bull.

Although he resonated to the alienation expressed in heavy metal songs, he was far from unhappy with his own life. Quite the contrary. This, and his general wholesomeness, sometimes made him feel out of place among other heavy metal fans, particularly at concerts.

I'm always in a good mood. . . . I don't walk around [calling people names]. I just go to the show 'cause I like the music. And it bothers me when people walk around calling me names, saying I'm not cool because I'm not wearing black.

Nevertheless, he thoroughly enjoyed going to concerts and purging his anger and aggression through slamdancing there. "[Slamdancing] is always to have a good time," he explained. "It's all fun, a way to release your aggressions if you're really upset. You get hurt, you get bruises, but it's such a good time." For Brian, heavy metal music was good-time music, the soundtrack of fun.

"When I'm really happy, I just put in metal and it just takes you away," he said. "It always makes me really energetic and happy and stuff. [Some of it is] really gloomy-sounding. And I can see why you'd listen to it if you have problems. But whenever I listen to it, it gets me so excited."

For many metalheads, there is at best an uneasy truce between them and their parents over the music, with the parents disliking it but not forbidding them to listen to it. In Brian's case, however, his parents actually promoted and encouraged his interest in heavy metal.

> *They're supportive. They don't get into it or anything, but they have no problems with it. When I'm in the car with them, if I want to put in an Anthrax tape or something, they're fine. My dad used to go to all the shows with me. And when we used to have to camp out for tickets he used to wake me up at four o'clock in the morning and take me down to [the record store] and wait with me. He went to every show with me until about a year and a half ago. Until they started letting me go by myself, he'd take me. And he's always calling people to try to get me stuff. He called [a guitar company] and got me tickets and back- stage passes for Slayer.*

If all this solicitude was intended by his parents to win their son's affection and admiration, it had certainly worked. "They're great. The best. [We get along] incredibly well. Occasionally we ar- gue about something, but nothing serious. They support me 110 percent. They're behind everything I do." Later in the interview, he named his dad as one of the three people he admired most. "To be honest with you, I admire my dad a lot because he's just the best. He's the coolest guy in the world."

As noted in Chapter 3, Slayer, his favorite band, is considered to be one of the heavy metal bands that openly promotes satanism. Brian was well aware of this, but he dismissed the satanist aspects of their songs as innocuous, not worth worrying about.

> [Do you think there are satanic messages in their songs?] *It's just a concept. It's like [other rock groups] singing about sex. For some peo- ple, [the lyrics may affect them] if they have too many problems or something, but it hasn't affected me. [Critics of the music] say that by listening to "Hell Awaits" by Slayer, we're just going to go straight to*

the pits of hell and burn. And we're sitting there going, "I'm doing fine, Lady." They've taken it too far, I think.

So Brian, in spite of his fondness for Slayer, in spite of his enthusiasm for songs such as "Kill Again," did not seem in any way to be a menace to himself or the people around him. The grimness of the heavy metal ideology seemed to him to speak the truth about the condition of the world, but this alienation did not extend to his personal life. He had not turned away from the hope that the world holds the possibility of a good and happy life for him. On the contrary, he was full of optimism, "always in a good mood," wary of the corruptness of the world but fully expecting to find some happiness in it. He reported occasional high-speed driving and one episode of vandalism in the past year (see Summary Profile), but in these respects and others he was straighter and less reckless than most middle-class adolescent boys. He seemed proud of his straightness, all the more because he was straight as well as being a metalhead.

I don't drink or smoke or do drugs or anything. I'm really anti-all-that-stuff, which I'm really proud of. 'Cause everyone's always like, "You gotta do drugs if you listen to Slayer." That's a good one I hear all the time.

Summary profile: Brian

Age: 16
Race: White
Education: currently in 12th grade
Father's occupation: oil company executive
Mother's occupation: real estate agent
Family background: parents married, but for past year father has been working and living in New York, rest of family in Atlanta
Spent most of childhood in: San Francisco
Number of heavy metal recordings owned: 40–50
Favorite heavy metal group: Slayer, "no doubt"
Goals in ten years: be a heavy metal musician or own a music store
Political orientation: "I'm not much for politics."
Religious orientation: indifferent
Hobbies/leisure preferences: Spanish Club, baseball, collects baseball cards

Three people most admired: father, the band Metallica, Carl Yastrzemski (former baseball player)

Number of times in past year:

Driven a car under the influence of alcohol:	0
Driven a car over 80 miles per hour:	1
Driven a car greater than 20 mph over speed limit:	2–5
Had sex without contraception:	0
Had sex with someone not known well:	0
Used marijuana:	0
Used cocaine:	0
Used illegal drugs other than marijuana or cocaine:	0
Damaged or destroyed public or private property:	1
Shoplifted:	0

The Allure of Heavy Metal

The road of excess leads to the palace of wisdom.

—William Blake, nineteenth-century English artist, poet, and mystic

Passion paralyzes good taste, and makes its victim accept with rapture what a man in his senses would either laugh at or turn from with disgust.

—Thomas Mann, *Death in Venice*

The song analysis outlined in Chapter 3 indicates that heavy metal songs are overwhelmingly dominated by themes and moods that express the ugly and unhappy side of life. The world according to heavy metal is nasty, brutish, dangerous, corrupt. Nothing escapes this taint, not even sex and love. Moreover, there is no prospect, no hope even, that things will ever be any better. The lonely and courageous individual can resist and defy the forces of oppression that dominate the world, but he will never overthrow them, and he is likely to be crushed by them sooner rather than later.

These grim lyrical themes are reinforced by the music. The drums pound thunderously, the bass guitar rumbles like the growl of an angry beast, the lead guitar races madly as it piles dozens of notes into each measure, the vocalist shouts, screams, and roars with rage and agony. The combination of these sounds gives the music an apocalyptic quality. Even if you could not understand a word of the lyrics (and sometimes you cannot), the message would be clear: Things are falling apart, the center is disintegrating, mere anarchy is being loosed upon the world.

To the unbeliever, the nonmetalhead, the appeal of such music may be difficult to understand. What pleasure could there be in listening to music that is so gloomy and angry? People listen to music for the purpose of enjoyment, presumably. So what enjoyment could anyone find in listening to music that is deliberately abrasive and grinding, with lyrics that are relentlessly pessimistic? A number of valid answers could be offered to this question, because individual metalheads listen to heavy metal for different reasons and because most of them have more than one reason for listening to it. I'll be offering answers throughout this book, in relation to various aspects of their socialization. First, however, we will hear from the boys themselves. As we will see, when they speak of why they like heavy metal music, they often cite the musical talent and skill of the performers. They also talk about the high-sensation intensity of it; the extremes of volume, speed, and power that make the music so distasteful to many people are precisely what is attractive about it to many metalheads. Perhaps most of all there is the ideology of it, the ideology of alienation. To metalheads, heavy metal performers represent a rare authenticity in a corrupt world, and the ideology of alienation gives metalheads a way of making sense of that world. Paradoxically, they find meaning and consolation through sharing in a declaration that the world is meaningless and without consolation.

Beauty is in the ear of the beholder

For the most part we do not expect pop musicians to possess exceptional musical talent or to display extraordinary musical skill. Most people would not consider Madonna to have a great singing voice. Bruce Springsteen is not considered, perhaps even by himself, to be a great guitarist. Pop music has more to do with melody and personality than with musical excellence. It may come as a surprise, then, that when metalheads talk about why they like heavy metal music, they often mention the musical expertise of the performers. "Each member is a virtuoso of his instrument," Spencer said of Metallica. "Randy Rhoads [former guitarist for Ozzy Ozbourne] is my absolute hero," said Matt, unabashedly. "Yeah, I worship that guy, 'cause he's just the greatest guitarist ever. He was just an awesome musician. He's probably one of the best musicians who ever lived."

Scott, an aspiring guitar player like many of the metalheads, spoke of going to concerts for what amounted to a guitar lesson: "I've been to some real heavy concerts, like Slayer, where you're watching those guys and you say to yourself, 'That's amazing!' So I don't always go to a concert just to listen. I also go there to sit and observe, see how it's played. It's a lot like classical music, in a way, because there's so much to it." Reggie, too, finds a classical-level expertise in the guitarists he admires. "If you listen to any of [Metallica's] tapes, their arrangements are intensely technical. Their guitarist is so good, he plays some things that a lot of good violinists can't play."

What makes heavy metal songs seem complex and highly technical to its fans is that the guitar playing is often densely packed with notes and is extremely fast, not just for a few notes but for long stretches of a song. Speed is paramount, and speed is what impresses the metalheads most.

Metalheads greatly admire the musical skills of the performers. (Photo by Nick Romanenko)

"To watch guys play [the guitar] 192 miles an hour for ninety minutes is just amazing to me," said Marvin. "With a band like Dark Angel, it's *zip* for ninety minutes."

Their admiration of the speed at which the guitarists play brings to mind a story about the great pianist, Vladimir Horowitz, who was asked to teach a class for some aspiring young pianists. He walked in and sat down at the piano and played a piece at a breathtaking speed. When he had finished he turned to his wide-eyed audience and said, "That was easy." Then he proceeded to play a slow piece with delicious expressiveness. When he had finished he turned again to his audience and said, "*That* was hard." This kind of subtlety has no place in heavy metal music. To the metalheads, speed equals virtuosity. But they admire the guitar-playing skill that it takes to play at such a furious tempo, much as a lover of classical music might admire Horowitz.[1]

Appetite for sensation

As I described in Chapter 1, part of the appeal of heavy metal for the metalheads is the astonishingly high level of volume and force that characterizes the music, particularly in the concert experience. Metalheads love the grinding, pounding sensations of the music, they love the *intensity* of it. To them, a heavy metal concert is the sensory equivalent of war—without the bullets—and they find it exhilarating. It is the ultimate in sheer skull-pounding, body-wracking, roaring sensation, and to them it is an ecstatic experience.

The love of such intense sensations is not characteristic of all adolescents, but it is generally more acute during adolescence than at other stages of life. Adolescents, to a greater extent than people in other age groups, love experiences such as driving in a convertible with the top down, riding on roller coasters, traveling to strange places, and the like.[2] Enjoyment of these types of experiences is a reflection of the personality trait of *sensation seeking*, which is the degree of *novelty* and *intensity* of sensation a person prefers. People vary in the amount of novelty and intensity of sensation they find pleasurable. A high-sensation experience—watching a horror movie, for example, or jumping into a cold lake on a hot day—is likely to be experienced as deeply pleasurable by someone who is high in sensation seeking, whereas someone who is relatively low in sensation seeking would find the same experience unpleasant and disagreeable.

The musical combination of speed, roughness, and volume that is characteristic of the heavy metal sound makes for an orgy of auditory sensation, and the metalheads find it thrilling. Words for high sensation such as "intense," "fast," "energy," and "loudness" come up often when metalheads explain why they like the music. Almost all of the metalheads used terms like these when I asked them why they like heavy metal and which groups and songs they especially like. "I like 'Die by My Hand,' by Coronary," said Lew. Why? "It's really intense." TJ favors the band Megadeth. "They are so hard. I love them, man. The music, and the rhythm, real intense rhythm." Steve likes Slayer because they are "the hardest and fastest there is." Bob named "Whiplash," by Metallica, as one of his favorite songs. "It's just very fast, at a very high energy level, with lots of energy behind it." Jess likes metal because "it's aggressive; I just like the speed and the anger of it." "I love his electric guitar," Derek rhapsodized about his favorite heavy metal guitar player. "I mean, it's *screaming*." "In my car I listen to it really loud," said Peter; like most boys, he has to modify the volume a bit at home, at least when his parents are around. And when parents are not around, said Tommy, "I like it super loud. Let's shake the house." But the live performance is the ultimate in high sensation, surpassing anything the metalheads can create on their home stereos. "I like hearing groups live much better than on records," said Michael. "It's got more power to it." James likes going to concerts "just for the loudness."

The advances in sound technology that have taken place over the past half-century, both on the concert level and on the home stereo level, make possible the extraordinarily high-sensation sound of heavy metal. The sound of the electric guitar bites with exceptional precision, the drums pound with unprecedented force, the vocals are given an unearthly raw-ness. Most important of all is *volume*. At concerts the volume is awesome, body-shaking, but even on a relatively modest home stereo system these days a volume can be reached that will rattle the walls (and drive every-one else in the house to distraction). Heavy metal would be impossible without this technology. As Marvin put it, "Heavy metal is made to be played loud."

The novelty of the heavy metal sound is also part of the allure for some boys. What first attracted TJ about heavy metal was that "I'd never heard anything like it." Ron was drawn to Metallica because "it was just new when it came out and I really, really got into that." And as Henry recalled, "When I first heard it, I said, 'Wow!' I said, 'Hey, this is different. Not many people listen to it. Let's see what it's like.' And I started to enjoy it."

In some heavy metal songs the lyrics add to the high sensation of the songs. When the lyrics describe bizarre creatures or events of violence, they give the songs the quality of an auditory horror story or horror movie. Like heavy metal songs, horror stories and horror movies from Edgar Allan Poe to Stephen King often involve violence and portray a grim, dark, brutal world. Many heavy metal songs have this kind of hor-ror-story quality—Judas Priest's "Night Crawler," for example (see Chapter 3 for a description), in which a demonic character stalks and then kills an innocent victim. To portray such horror stories in the form of songs is not necessarily more insidious or objectionable than the print or movie form. In all these forms horror is appealing to some people for the same underlying reason: It is a high-sensation experience involving a sense of excitement, suspense, and physiological arousal, yet within safe boundaries and without any actual danger.

Understanding high sensation as part of the allure of heavy metal mu-sic helps explain why most metalheads are young and male: In general adolescents are higher in sensation seeking than adults are (although at every age there is variability among individuals), and males are higher than females.[3] Heavy metal music appeals to this hunger for high sensa-tion that many adolescent boys and young men possess. For most adults and most adolescent girls, the level of sensation in heavy metal music is far beyond the threshold at which sensation changes from pleasurable to disagreeable. For adolescent metalheads, however, that threshold is much higher, if not infinite, and heavy metal music fills their sensation-seeking appetites with an abundance of pleasurable sensations. To paraphrase the epigraphs that began this chapter, the musical excesses in heavy metal that cause most other people either to laugh or to turn away with disgust are the same ones that the metalheads find so enjoyable.

TABLE 4.1   Sample Sensation-Seeking Items

	Percent Answering "Yes"	
Item	Metalheads	Other Boys
I like to try new foods that I have never tasted before.	67	37
I would like to take off on a trip with no preplanned or definite routes or timetable.	74	51
I would like to try parachute jumping.	71	56
I prefer friends who are excitingly unpredictable.	64	33
People should dress in individual ways even if the effects are sometimes strange.	79	54
I like to have new and exciting experiences and sensations even if they are a little frightening, unconventional, or illegal.	80	58

This unusually strong desire for high sensation is expressed not only in their love of heavy metal but in a variety of aspects of their lives. Table 4.1 shows some examples of how they differed from other boys on various items from the scale of sensation seeking I used in the study.[4] Even compared to other adolescent boys (who are already higher in sensation seeking than most adults or adolescent girls), metalheads score higher. They indicate a greater desire for novel and intense experiences, from trying new foods to dressing in unusual ways to parachute jumping.

The ideology of alienation

There is more to the appeal of heavy metal music than the appreciation of the performers' playing skill, more than the high-sensation pleasure of the music. There is also the ideology of it. Heavy metal music is not simply a musical preference to most of the boys who like it, the way a person might have a preference for, say, dance music or jazz. It is not merely a diversion, but something that both shapes and reflects their view of the

world and of themselves. They are called "metalheads" or "headbangers," and they call themselves by these titles as well, with a certain ironic
pride. These are ideological labels at least as much as they are a declaration of musical taste.

As the song analysis in Chapter 3 illustrates, the ideology of heavy
metal is one of pervasive alienation. Ties to family, lovers, nation, and religion are held in suspicion and contempt, and violence is often either
feared or threatened by the singer. But this alienation is carried with pride
and defiance by the performers and their fans. It takes courage, in their
eyes, to expose the lies and ugliness of the world as it is. This courage is,
in part, what defines heavy metal for them. Above all else heavy metal
songs and performers must be *authentic,* in the sense that they present the
unvarnished truth about what the world is like, in all its rottenness. One
way metalheads distinguish the genuine, authentic heavy metal performers from the imitators is that the authentic metal performer loudly and
vehemently spouts the ideology of alienation, whereas imitators, the
"poseurs," sing songs about frivolous topics such as partying and the joys
of promiscuity.

True metal songs contain the authenticity that is sought by the metalheads, in the messages of the lyrics. These lyrics seem to the metalheads
to speak the truth about society. "Heavy metal gets down to the issues,"
said Rich. "A lot of it's about the hardships of life." Barry, like many of the
boys, sees the world he is growing up in as having a multitude of grave
problems. To him, heavy metal songs serve an important function, expos-
ing the corruptions of society that people need to hear about, whether
they like it or not. "I think one of the reasons [critics] are so hard on it is
that it really tells the truth. It tells the truth about everything, and people
don't want to hear it." Jack offered a similar view: "[Opponents of the
music] don't want reality facts, don't want to look at what's going on in
our world."

Metalheads, by listening to the songs and by thinking of themselves as
metalheads, as adherents of the messages of the songs, see themselves as
sharing in the declaration of these messages. There is a tendency among
adolescents to notice, in a way they did not when they were younger, the
imperfections of adult society and the hypocrisy inherent in much of
adult life.[5] Through heavy metal music, they see themselves as participating in a brave effort to expose this falseness.

Heavy metal performers declare their authenticity not only through
their songs but through their appearance, and many fans do as well. The
long hair, tattoos, earrings, and other trappings of the performers are
ways of declaring, and of signifying to their metalhead followers, that
they care little for the societal convention of how men should look, and
little for the society that this convention represents. For metalheads who

model their own appearance after the performers—and not all metal-heads do, but some do—this is a way of declaring not only their admiration for the performers and their solidarity with other heavy metal fans, but also of declaring that they, too, are authentic. They, too, are not afraid to expose boldly the corruptions of their society.

The ideological quality of heavy metal is evident in how the metal-heads speak of their favorite performers. It is evident that authenticity is of primary importance. "I admire the guys in Metallica just because they've been around for six years and they're never dressed up, they've never changed their music," said Brian. "Never selling out or giving in. Just being themselves." As much as the boys admire the musical skill of the performers, a heavy metal hero must have not only musical expertise but personal integrity as well. "I really like Lars Ulrich [the drummer for Metallica]," said Jess. "He's a genius. And it's not just his style of drum-ming that I like. It's also that he's a really smart guy, and down-to-earth." Musicianship and integrity are expected to go together. In fact, musician-ship is seen as one reflection of integrity. "Randy Rhoads [former guitarist for Ozzy Ozbourne] has been a really big influence on me," said Mark. Why? "Just for what he stood for and everything. One of his quotes that I remember is like, 'My strength is my determination and that's why I keep getting better.' I thought that was really something. And he was totally dedicated to what he did."

Metalheads despise the poseurs, the bands and performers that claim to be part of the heavy metal clan but are not legitimate. Poseurs have a carefully contrived image, designed to make them look like and sound like a heavy metal band, but the image is false. They are only pretending to be heavy metal heroes in order to enrich themselves. The metalheads despise them with all the contempt that true believers always have for compromisers and hypocrites. Spencer contrasted the integrity of a true metal band with the hypocrisy of the poseurs: "[The performers in Metallica are] just really down-to-earth guys who are not image-con-scious like the Bon Jovis and Poisons of the world. They concentrate on their music."

In contrast to the poseurs, metalheads see the performers in the true metal bands as having no use for gimmickry. These performers believe in the music, according to the metalheads, and everything else, even the huge sums of money they get from playing it, is irrelevant. Jason said his favorite metal bands were "not into complete commercialism, you know what I'm saying?" One of the reasons Peter gave for liking heavy metal bands is that "they're not just going in there for the money."

Metalheads see the performers as paragons of integrity, unconcerned with image. As is often the case with true believers, the metalheads over-look the flaws in their leaders, flaws that may seem obvious to the more skeptical observer. Such an observer might quickly notice that the performers in heavy metal bands look remarkably similar to one another in spite of their professed contempt for presenting a contrived image. Virtually all of them have long hair, well past their shoulders. Virtually all of them wear either leather or denim or both, and many of them wear gaudy necklaces as well. Multiple tattoos are obligatory. There is even a tendency for the guitar players in the different bands to swing their hair around as they play, with torsos leaning forward, knees bent, legs stretching wide.

It may also seem somewhat puzzling to an unbeliever that metalheads see heavy metal performers as having no concern for money, in light of the fact that metalheads have all had the experience of paying twenty dollars and more for concert tickets, and many have also paid the exorbitant prices charged for heavy metal t-shirts, concert programs, and assorted paraphernalia. The metalheads, however, see no contradiction in this, and no compromise of virtue.

The puzzle of alienation

In sum, the reasons for the appeal of heavy metal music include admiration for the musical talent and skill of the performers, enjoyment of the intense sensations of the music, and a fervent belief in the ideology of alienation expressed in heavy metal songs. The metalheads' embrace of the ideology of alienation is of particular interest because of what it suggests about the experience of growing up as an adolescent in our time. The provocative question is, Why did this ideology suddenly become attractive to millions of adolescents (mostly boys) in America, Europe, and around the world in the 1980s and early 1990s? Why, in a time of the greatest comfort and affluence the world has ever known, have so many young people come to see life as so grim? And why has this taken place in precisely those countries in which the level of comfort and affluence is highest, and not merely among working-class boys but among middle- and upper-middle-class boys as well?

In the course of the next several chapters I will explore the various sources of alienation in metalheads' families, schools, and communities, as well as their alienation from traditional religion. For many of the metalheads, their alienation is partly rooted in one or more of these sources. As we will see, one reason the metalheads respond so fervently to the ideology of alienation is that it is reflected in their experience. Its portrayal of the world as a lonely place, where ties to others cannot be trusted and the meaning of it all is difficult to fathom, is all too familiar from their own lives.

PROFILE

Spencer

The first thing you noticed about Spencer was his bat tattoo. You could hardly miss it; it was spread across the top of his chest, with a six-inch wingspan. Another tattoo, of a guitar, decorated his right arm. He had facial hair of several days' growth, and he was wearing a blue baseball cap, on backward in the current adolescent style. He had come to the interview directly from his job as a furniture packer, and he was dressed in work clothes: blue jeans and a light-blue t-shirt. He had an easy smile and an affable way about him.

Spencer was living a reckless, chaotic, disordered life—and loving it. His explanation of how he came to be living in Atlanta is illustrative.

The whole story behind me moving to Atlanta two months ago was that I took my girlfriend to a concert at the Center Stage [a small concert venue in Atlanta]. It ended up with me getting left in Atlanta by my friends and getting fired from the job I'd had in Athens [Georgia]. Me and my friends wanted to go to that concert in Atlanta. We didn't have a car, so we borrowed this girl's car that one of my friends knew. We had a load of furniture we had to deliver in Alabama the next day, so we were gonna go to the concert, come back [to Athens], get in the truck, and go to Alabama to deliver. Well, on the way down there we started getting real drunk. When we got to the concert, me and my girlfriend started fighting, and we split up, and I tried to get away from her, and I ended up getting lost from my friends. Brian, who was the driver, had to get the furniture so he went ahead and drove back to Athens. On his way back, he got a DUI [arrested for drunk driving], so there went his truck-driving job. I was working for him, so there went my job. The other guy who was with us also worked there and he lost his job, and my girlfriend got in big trouble, so I decided just to stay away from all that and just stay up here for a while.

For him, one of the attractions of attending a heavy metal concert was the chaos of it, the absence of restraint, especially during
slamdancing.

> *[Slamdancing is] real good fun, believe it or not, if you like that sort of*
> *thing. It's just such an intense thing to get in. Nothing you could pos-*
> *sibly do while [slamdancing] could be socially unacceptable. You could*
> *walk up and pound someone in the face, and it's all in good fun.*

Listening to heavy metal at other times also provided an aggressive release for him. "There are just times when you get the urge
to hear some thrash [metal]," he said, and those tended to be times
when he was "extremely mad at the world, not at any person in
particular." Another reason why heavy metal appealed to him was
that he admired the musical expertise of heavy metal performers,
and he took them as models for his own guitar-playing aspirations. He had high hopes for his prospects as a professional guitarist. Ten years from now, he expected to be showered in heavy
metal glory, "playing the Omni [an 18,000-seat arena in Atlanta]
with a metal band."

It would be a mistake to dismiss this too easily as mere adolescent grandiosity; it probably was, but all successful pop musicians
must have begun with a similar dream. In Spencer's case, he did
seem to be more serious and musically knowledgeable than many
of the other boys in the study who stated similar dreams. He said
he was learning to sight-read music, described classical music as
"a strong influence on me, even in the heavy stuff," and had
bought a four-track reel-to-reel tape recorder to learn the basics of
recording music. However, he was not now and had never been in
a working band.

His family life had not been smooth. His parents divorced when
he was seven, and his mom had difficulty with Spencer as a single
parent. Things worsened as he entered adolescence—just about
the time he discovered heavy metal, which may or may not be a
coincidence. "About the time I turned thirteen, my mom relin-
quished all control over me," he said. "She realized she couldn't
control me." His relations with his father were no better than with
his mother. "We just can't stand living together," he said.

A similar unruliness was characteristic of Spencer's school experience. He could not tolerate the passive routine of it, the lack of

stimulation, and this led him to frequent conflicts with teachers. Although he had shown signs of creativity, both in and out of school—he had written many songs and during high school he had written "some short stories and half-finished novels"—it was, as he might have acknowledged, an undisciplined creativity. He had shown enough promise as a writer to be in a "gifted and talented" writing class in high school, but he dropped it when he "decided that sitting at a typewriter was too boring."

Strange as it might seem for a kid with a bat tattoo on his chest, he described himself as "a very firmly believing Christian. I'm not a very good one, but I do actually believe." But his religious faith was characterized by the same untamed quality, the same indiscipline. He had only attended church once in the past two years. He had a somewhat romantic view of how he might eventually practice his religious faith. "I've made it my objective that when I finally get to the top, where I think I'll be as popular as I can get playing [heavy metal] music, I'll express [my Christianity] in my music."

For him to reach that goal, or any of his other goals, he would have to learn much in the way of self-restraint and self-discipline. He was enjoying his chaotic life in the present, and he was making the most of the kind of hiatus that adolescence provides for experimenting, for reckless adventuring, that is condoned and even in a way admired by American society as a whole. Even his broken relationships with his parents and his poor record in school did not seem to trouble him. Eventually, however, the hiatus of adolescence would be over and living a chaotic life would no longer be seen by others as a healthy sowing of wild oats but as intolerable immaturity. What would become of him then?

Summary profile: Spencer

Age: 19
Race: White
Education: high school graduate
Current occupation: furniture packer/mover
Father's occupation: philosophy professor
Mother's occupation: legal secretary
Family background: parents divorced when he was seven years old, mother
    "couldn't control me," he and father "can't stand living together"
Spent most of childhood in: Arkansas

Number of heavy metal recordings owned: about 200
Favorite heavy metal groups: Metallica
Goals in ten years: play guitar in a successful heavy metal band
Political orientation: "no interest whatsoever"
Religious orientation: "I'm a very firmly believing Christian"
Hobbies/leisure preferences: electric guitar
Number of times in past year:

Driven a car under the influence of alcohol:	>10
Driven a car over 80 miles per hour:	11–20
Driven a car greater than 20 mph over speed limit:	21–50
Had sex without contraception:	>10
Had sex with someone not known well:	6–10
Used marijuana:	0
Used cocaine:	>10
Used illegal drugs other than marijuana or cocaine:	>10
Damaged or destroyed public or private property:	>10
Shoplifted:	1

The Effects of Heavy Metal

Man's tragic destiny [is that] he must desperately justify himself as an object of primary value in the universe; he must stand out, be a hero, make the biggest possible contribution to world life, show that he counts. . . . The crisis of modern society is precisely that the youth no longer feel heroic in the plan for action that their culture has set up.

—**Ernest Becker,** *The Denial of Death*

Music has charms to soothe a savage breast.

—**William Congreve,** *The Mourning Bride* **(1697)**

One of the reasons heavy metal music has received so much public attention and debate over the past decade is that some critics hear in it not just obnoxious music but an incitement to antisocial behavior. It is not difficult to find such incitements in the lyrics, as we saw in Chapter 3. Violence, defying authority, breaking the norms and rules of society— these are common themes in heavy metal songs, and it could be argued (as the critics do) that these themes promote behavior that is disruptive to the rest of society, behavior such as violence toward self and others, sexual promiscuity, drug use and drunkenness, and the destruction of property. Even if the songs do not specifically advocate these types of behavior, they could be said to promote them because they advocate, on a more general level, an alienated individualism that rejects any restraints on behavior.

People who suspect the songs of being guilty in this respect naturally scrutinize metalheads for evidence that their suspicions are valid. The media aid them in this process by helpfully pointing out when someone under investigation for a sensational crime is also a fan of heavy metal music. In 1991, for example, a New Hampshire schoolteacher was convicted of persuading her high school student lover to murder her husband. It was noted numerous times that she was a big fan of heavy metal, and she had once been a disc jockey on a radio station where she called herself "The Maiden of Metal." The musical preferences of the actual murderer went unmentioned.

Heavy metal and reckless behavior

Not even the severest critics claim that heavy metal turns all of its listeners into potential murderers. The questions to be answered are more modest, although still serious. Are metalheads more reckless than other adolescents? And, if so, can heavy metal music be said to cause or at least contribute to their recklessness?

The first question can be answered easily. The metalheads in this study clearly are more reckless than other boys. As Table 5.1 shows, this is true in a variety of areas.[1] They more frequently drive while intoxicated or at high speeds. They more frequently have sex without contraception or with someone they do not know well. They are more likely to use marijuana, cocaine, or other illegal drugs. They vandalize and shoplift more often.

It seems easy to conclude that the answer to the second question is also affirmative: Heavy metal music causes metalheads to behave recklessly. The songs contain antisocial themes, and adolescent boys who listen to them have higher rates of antisocial behavior; ergo, listening to heavy metal music leads to antisocial behavior. This would be the simple conclusion to be drawn from Table 5.1, but it would also be simplistic. I would argue, instead, that metalheads are attracted both to heavy metal and to reckless behavior for a common underlying reason: the high-sen-

TABLE 5.1   Rates of Reckless Behavior

Type of behavior	Percent at Least Once in Past Year	
	Metalheads	Other Boys
Driving while drunk	44	17
Driving over 80 mph	73	50
Driving > 20 mph over speed limit	77	61
Sex without contraception	30	22
Sex with someone not known well	43	20
Marijuana use	50	13
Cocaine use	19	0
Other illegal drug use	29	6
Vandalism	54	40
Shoplifting	41	23

sation thrill of the experience.[2] Adolescent boys who are high in sensation seeking tend to be attracted to heavy metal music and also tend to have higher rates of reckless behavior, because both heavy metal music and reckless behavior provide intense and novel sensations. As a consequence, boys who like heavy metal music are generally more reckless than other boys, and this *correlation* may make it look to some observers as if heavy metal *causes* reckless/antisocial behavior. However, correlation should not be misinterpreted here as causation. Enjoyment of heavy metal music and enjoyment of reckless behavior tend to be found in the same boys, not because heavy metal music causes reckless behavior but because both experiences reflect an enjoyment of intense and novel sensations.

Recall that one of the principal attractions of heavy metal music is the novelty and intensity of the sensations it provides, and also that metalheads are higher than nonmetalheads in sensation seeking. As Chapter 4 showed, when metalheads describe why they like the music, they tend to use words like "intense," "speed," "energy," "exciting," and "power." For metalheads, it is a thrilling, absorbing experience to listen to the music as it blasts out of their home stereo or as they participate in the ecstatic ritual of the concert.

Look at the way they describe their participation in reckless behavior and you find the same attraction to the intensity and the excitement of it. Nick, for example, described the thrill of driving extremely fast, at night—with the headlights off. "I love to drive fast. But after awhile driving fast just wasn't doing it any more, so I started driving without the lights on, going about ninety on country roads. I even got a friend to do it. We'd go cruising down country roads, turn off the lights, and just fly. It was incredible. We'd go as fast as we could, [and] at night with no lights it feels like you're just flying."

Many young men revel like this in the power of high-speed driving and find a kind of intoxication in the sensation of moving at high speeds. This is especially true for metalheads, with their unusually acute enjoyment of high-sensation experiences. But as Table 5.1 shows, driving at high speeds is a common form of recklessness among nonmetalheads as well. For adolescent boys in the American middle class, a car is the quickest and easiest transport to excitement and adventure, to sensation-seeking intensity. Unfortunately, this accessible and attractive route to fun is also all-too-easily lethal; stories like Nick's help explain why automobile accidents are the leading cause of death for young men aged 15–24[3] and why young men of that age have the highest rate of accidents and fatalities of any group in the United States.[4]

High sensation is also part of the attraction of other reckless adventures. Sexual activity involves sensations that are intense and, for adolescents, novel as well; risky and unusual sexual experiences are still higher in novelty and intensity. Trying illegal drugs results in novel forms of consciousness, so that some adolescents wish to try them "to see what it would be like." Common adolescent crimes like shoplifting and vandalism carry the thrill arising from the possibility of being caught in the act, and vandalism offers the additional thrill of sheer destructiveness. Rich described how "we used to load up the back of this guy's car with bricks, and we'd drive through the neighborhoods, and hang out the windows, and whenever we saw one of those wooden mail boxes we'd just chuck the brick at it and watch it just crumble in the street. We thought that was the *best*. Then we'd go back the next day to look at the damage. We'd go through the neighborhoods, 'Look at that one, man!' [Why did you do it?] It was so fun!" Like high-speed driving, these other types of recklessness appeal to many adolescent boys but especially to metalheads, with their greater tendency for sensation seeking.

One sometimes gets a sense, hearing these tales, of young men who have too little to do. They have reached a near-adult level of physical, sexual, and intellectual maturity, and yet there is no place for them to exercise their capacities, no useful work to occupy them.[5] More to the point, there is nothing *exciting* offered to them, no culturally structured adventures awaiting, to fill up this immense capacity they feel for excitement and adventure. Young men in other times and other places who have this heightened appetite for sensation can go off to war, or set out to explore an unknown land, or are so occupied with adult work that it consumes all of their energy and attention. Young men in our time must create their own adventures. And without a culturally defined setting and stage for putting their sensation-seeking energy into socially approved activities that hold the promise of excitement and heroic adventure, that energy often takes undisciplined, antisocial, and socially disruptive forms.

Music has charms to soothe the angry metalhead

I have argued that it is sensation seeking, not heavy metal music, that is the boys' primary motivation for reckless behavior. Sensation seeking may underlie both their attraction to heavy metal music and their enjoyment of reckless behavior. However, even more persuasive evidence that heavy metal music does not cause boys to be reckless comes from what the boys themselves say about the effects of the music.

It is not difficult to see why many adults have expressed alarm at heavy metal songs and why the songs have even been accused of leading to murder and suicide in some widely publicized cases. The characteristic sentiments of the songs are sadness and (especially) anger, and there is a certain compelling logic to supposing that if you listen to sad songs you're likely to become sad, if you listen to angry songs they may make you angry, and that while in the grip of these emotions you may do something that is destructive or self-destructive. If you are already in a dark mood when you listen to such songs, it is easy to suppose that your mood would be likely to become still darker.

It does seem to be true that metalheads seek out heavy metal music when they are in a dark mood. When asked whether they listen to heavy metal music more often when they are in any particular mood, 48 percent of the metalheads said they listen to it especially when they are angry.[6] The sources of anger they mentioned were those you might expect for adolescent boys: conflicts with parents, conflicts with friends, conflicts with girlfriends, difficulties in school. An additional 7 percent of the boys mentioned other negative emotions, such as anxiety or sadness, when asked whether they listen to heavy metal music when in a particular mood.

On the surface it is not surprising that boys should listen to heavy metal especially when they are angry. Heavy metal is, after all, angry music. But what mood does it then put them in? It might be expected that the songs would only inflame the anger, like putting a match to a pile of explosives. Is it possible for angry music to have any other effect than to incite and inflame anger?

The answer is surprising: Heavy metal music characteristically has the effect of *calming them down*, of purging their anger rather than inflaming it. Over half of the metalheads who said they listen to it especially when in a negative mood also reported a cathartic effect of this kind, an effect of relieving their anger, unhappiness, or anxiety. Many of them consciously *use* the music to purge themselves of these negative emotions.[7] "It's sort of like taking a tranquilizer," said Henry.

The boys described this process, of how listening to the music purges their anger, with remarkable insight and sometimes with an almost clinical detachment. Steve described how the music stirs the anger up but in doing so washes it out: "It seems to escalate the anger when I'm listening to it, pumps up the adrenaline, but at the same time it's a release of anger as well," he observed. "You turn it on and it pumps you up, but when it's over you feel more relaxed."

Ben described listening to heavy metal as an alternative to more violent ways of releasing his anger.

Sometimes I'm upset and I like to put on heavy metal. It kind of releases the aggression I feel. Instead of going out and getting all mad at somebody I can just drive along, put a tape in, and turn it up. It puts me in a better mood. It's a way to release some of your pressures, instead of going out and starting a fight with somebody, you know? Or taking it out on your parents or your cat or something like that.

Mark was an interesting variation on the theme of catharsis. He used the music to purge anxiety, nervousness, rather than anger. Hyperactive as a boy, he still often found himself with too much energy at the end of the day. So, before going to sleep, he would lie in bed and listen to heavy metal on his stereo, which would have the effect of relaxing him and preparing him for sleep. It may be hard to understand how listening to songs like "Bodily Dismemberment" (one of his favorites) could be relaxing, but for him apparently it is.

Some boys even said they use particular songs or groups precisely for the purpose of purging negative emotions. Rob said he listened to the group Testament "to relieve anger," as if he were describing his use of a prescription drug. Jack described "Trapped Under Ice" by Metallica as being "good for frustrated depression." James said that listening to "In My Darkest Hour" by Megadeth makes him and his friends feel better about "girls stomping on our egos." When Randy is upset, just thinking about his favorite heavy metal songs is enough to calm him down.

> If I'm really upset or something's really bothering me and I just have to calm down, there's a metal tape I listen to. I don't even have to listen to the tape itself, I can just think about the songs and I can usually calm myself down if I'm really worked up.

Scott and other boys spoke of listening to the "harder" metal (that is, angrier) when they were feeling especially intense anger. "If I'm really ticked off, I would listen more to the hard stuff. The hard stuff kind of calms me down. They're spitting out all these problems on the tape, so you figure yours aren't so bad." And in spite of the hopeless, even nihilistic quality of the lyrics of most heavy metal songs, not one of the boys— not a single one—said that the songs make him feel hopeless or even sad.

What is surprising about this is not that music, in general, can have a soothing effect on people. Other studies have indicated that adolescents cite "listening to music" as their most preferred way of coping with anger, sadness, or anxiety,[8] and no doubt many adults would, too. Nor is this something new, a characteristic only of modern, amplified popular music.[9] In the biblical story over 3,000 years old, mad King Saul finds that the only effective remedy for his imagined terrors is to listen to the music of the harp as it is played by young David. But heavy metal is not harp music. Although it makes sense that soft, delicate, harmonious music has a soothing effect on many people, it is striking that metalheads find their music soothing even though it is as aggressive, abrasive, and loud as it could possibly be.

The cathartic effect of heavy metal is experienced not only in listening to recorded songs but also at concerts. In describing the release of aggression that takes place at concerts, the metalheads talk especially about slamdancing. The term is descriptive: They literally slam into each other. It is a physical expression of the anger of the music, and through it the metalheads release their own anger.

Steve described it as "mainly a release of aggression, tension, stress. Trying to get as wild as you can without killing yourself." Short and gaunt, he was living proof that you don't have to be large and muscular to take your chances in the slamdancing pit. It is true, however, that girls are rarely bold or foolish enough to slamdance with the boys. It is all boys, adolescent boys and young men abandoning themselves to an undirected outburst of anger. But although it is undirected, it is also controlled, in the sense that it is being expressed in the slamdancing pit and not elsewhere. Thus slamdancing functions in much the same way as listening to heavy metal music: Both experiences purge metalheads' anger and help them keep it under control at other times. Nick spoke for many of the boys as well as from personal experience when he said of slamdancing, "It beats going home and kicking your stereo over, or beating your best friend up."

In slamdancing the emphasis is on the "slam" rather than the "dance"; calling it a dance seems almost ironic, as there is no pattern or form to it. And yet it *is* a dance in the sense that there is an element of play to it. There is a great deal of aggression in it, but the aggression remains within certain boundaries. Erik described it as "just energetic and you're just in contact with a whole bunch of people and everybody's jumping into everybody else. But it's a good, fun, wholesome group activity." Everyone participating *expects* to slam and be slammed, so no one takes offense. "It's like a huge group fight, except no one's fighting," explained Spencer, "and in fact what's amazing is that all this goes on and no fights erupt out of it." Brian implied a shared understanding, among the metalheads, of the limits and purposes of slamdancing: "When parents look at it, they say 'Oh my God, they're killing each other.' But it's not like that when you're there. It's just a bunch of friends that are into the same music, having fun." A person may get slightly injured in the course of it, but this is considered not so much a deterrent from slamdancing as a badge of manly honor and another incentive to participate. As Mark put it, "I didn't do a good job if I don't come away with at least a scratch or a bloody nose."

The combination of the models of unrestraint exhibited by the performers, the outpouring of aggression experienced by the metalheads as they

Slamdancing: "It's like a huge group fight, except no one's fighting." (Photo by Nick Romanenko)

listen to intensely aggressive music at a towering volume, and the mob psychology of a large number of people pressed into a confined space would seem inherently to carry the potential for anarchy. Considering the volatility of this mixture, it is remarkable that the aggression remains within the relatively harmless boundaries of slamdancing.[10]

Heavy metal dreams

Relief of anger, frustration, sadness, and other negative emotions is perhaps the most notable effect that heavy metal music has on boys who listen to it, but it is not the only one. In addition, the love for heavy metal affects many of the boys in their choice of a career path. More precisely, many of them look onstage at the concert performers and see *themselves*, an alluring vision of their own future. They plan to be involved in heavy metal music in one way or another, and they are actively planning their lives with that goal in mind.

I did not anticipate this. I included the question "What do you see yourself doing in ten years?" in the interview in order to get some idea of how they imagined their lives after adolescence, presumably after their enthusiasm for heavy metal music had waned. As it turned out, the question revealed that many of the boys see their adolescence as continuing indefinitely, in their lives as heavy metal stars. A "career" in heavy metal offers a possible way of avoiding the drudgery characteristic of much middle-class adult work. "I need to see a list of all the jobs you can get playing the guitar, because I really enjoy it," said Matt. "I don't want to have to go to work thinking, 'Oh, God.'" Many of them genuinely believe that heavy metal stardom is what the future holds for them; this is their sincere hope and their earnest desire. "I want to be a guitarist in a band," said Tommy of his plan for his life ten years from now. "I'll be a musician," said Jason, "playing heavy metal." Altogether, 40 percent of the metalheads said they expected to be doing something related to music in ten years (compared to only 8 percent in the comparison group), and in most cases this involved performing heavy metal music before large audiences. For Ron, the answer to the question of how he saw himself ten years from now was simple: "Onstage. Live. In a heavy metal band."

One of the distinguishing characteristics of adolescent development is the grandiosity of adolescent thinking.[11] There is a tendency among adolescents to overmagnify their own powers and their own place in the scheme of things, to imagine the future as an unbroken path to the fulfillment of their dreams. Final limitations have not yet been set on their abilities; they have not yet tried and failed or come up short in many of the areas of life they aspire to succeed in. For adolescent metalheads, it is easy and fun for them to imagine, at age fourteen or seventeen or twenty-one, that heavy metal lightning will strike them and they will be lifted to a life of fame and glory as a heavy metal star. Many of them have learned to play the guitar or some other instrument, and this feeds the fantasy, this bolsters the credibility of the dream in their minds. They have not yet collided with the reality of how crowded the field is, how many other young men are grasping for the same goal, how much work and sacrifice and talent and good fortune it would require of them.

Another aspect of this adolescent grandiosity, this adolescent egocentrism, is the belief that you are the center of a universe, that the people around you are intensely preoccupied with everything you are doing, thinking, and feeling. David Elkind uses the term "the imaginary audience" to describe this,[12] and it is a term that is especially apt when applied to the metalheads. The scene they witness at concerts is like a fulfillment of the ultimate adolescent fantasy: You are the object of fervent adoration from a huge audience whose attention is entirely focused on you. It is not surprising that they find it so easy to imagine themselves in the role of the performers, since the whole scene incorporates a fantasy so common to the adolescent imagination.

Most metalheads with a heavy metal dream had an alternative career in mind in case that dream failed to materialize, but the alternative also frequently involved music. Brian hoped to be a heavy metal performer, but if that did not work out he thought he might end up owning a music store. Derek also hoped to be in a heavy metal band, but as an alternative he thought he might produce albums for heavy metal bands, and he was planning to enroll in a school for music production. Reggie, who currently writes about heavy metal for his high school newspaper, was anticipating a career writing books and articles on heavy metal music and musicians. Nick, an artist, had hopes of owning his own business, doing art work for heavy metal bands and other types of pop music performers. Still, these alternatives were mentioned by boys who suspected they did not have the musical talent to make it as performers. Those who believed they had musical talent saw themselves as performers.

Their intense identification with heavy metal performers, and the dream of achieving heavy metal stardom themselves, leads many metalheads to learn to play a musical instrument. Quite a remarkable proportion of the metalheads in this study (76 percent) said that they play some kind of musical instrument (electric guitar, for most), compared to only 35 percent of the boys in the comparison group. Thus, learning to play an instrument seems to be another effect of their enthusiasm for heavy metal music.[13] In addition, one-third of the metalheads said they were in a heavy metal band or had been in the past. For most of them, however, the goal of being a heavy metal star is more a romantic dream than a serious ambition. Although many of them spoke of being in a band or having been in one in the past or wishing to be in one, not one of them was currently in a band that was performing and getting paid for it.

Identification with heavy metal performers and dreams of heavy metal glory were also evident in the boys' responses to the question of whom they most admire. Asked to name three people, 50 percent of the metalheads named at least one heavy metal performer. In contrast, only 14 percent of the boys in the comparison group named a musician among the three people they most admired.

It is not difficult to understand the lure for adolescent boys of this fantasy of being a heavy metal star: riches, fame, and the adulation of millions, including many attractive young women. On one hand, one could argue that the fantasy does no harm at a time when they are in the process of forming an identity, when their own abilities and inclinations, and how these fit with the roles available to them in their society, still may not be evident to them. Because their broad socialization does not direct them into any specific adult role, they are allowed to experiment with (and dream of) a number of different possibilities, among them the possibility of being a heavy metal performer. On the other hand, it might be pointed out that identifying with the antisocial images of the performers does not bode well for the formation of character in adolescent fans of heavy metal music. It may be worth keeping in mind that the adolescents of the 1950s did not end up with adult personalities resembling Elvis Presley and James Dean.

However, there is a more subtle and perhaps more serious concern at issue here than the possibility that metalheads might grow into adulthood emulating heavy metal stars. It is the danger the great sociologist Emile Durkheim warned about a century ago: that young people who are socialized with a minimum of restraint may come to have expectations for their lives that are so exalted that reality cannot possibly satisfy them.[14] For a metalhead who expects to live the life of a rich, acclaimed heavy metal star—and whose expectations are formed not by the reality of that life but by the idealized way the boy has imagined it—working any ordinary job is likely to seem like a great disappointment. The danger for the metalheads is that, for those who fail to fulfill their heavy metal dreams, the result may be an even deeper alienation than they are already experiencing.

Socialization and the effects of heavy metal

What can we say, then, about the effects of heavy metal music on its fans? Given that the metalheads in this study reported consistently and independently that listening to heavy metal music has the effect of purging their anger and other negative emotions, and given that none of them said that the music incites them to aggressiveness or other antisocial behavior, it is difficult to make a case that the music is harmful to them or harmful to society because of the effects it has on the metalheads. It becomes difficult, too, to make a case for banning or otherwise restricting access to the music. Ironically, it would seem to make more sense to prescribe a steady program of listening to heavy metal music for boys who have a proclivity toward antisocial behavior, so that their aggressive tendencies might be purged harmlessly by the music instead of being taken out in disruptive ways on the people around them.

But what about the correlation between listening to heavy metal music and behaving recklessly? What about the fact that adolescent boys who like heavy metal are more likely to drive while drunk and at high speeds, have sex promiscuously and without contraception, use drugs, shoplift, and vandalize (not to mention many other varieties of recklessness)? The link between heavy metal music and reckless behavior is sensation seeking. Adolescent boys who have an especially large appetite for intensity and novelty of experience are attracted to the speed, roughness, and sheer volume of heavy metal music as well as to the risk, drama, and danger of reckless behavior.

But sensation seeking is not an immutable force that must find expression regardless of the characteristics of the social environment. People differ in the strength of their sensation-seeking tendency, probably innately, but the extent to which the tendency is actually expressed, and the form of its expression, depend on the restrictiveness of their socialization.[15] As discussed in Chapter 2, the majority culture in the United States is notable for its broad socialization—for how little children and adolescents are restricted and for how much they are encouraged toward individualism and self-expression. This is true of most parents, but it is also true of the other sources of socialization: Friends, schools, communities, the media, the legal system, and the cultural belief system in the American middle class all generally promote the individualism of broad socialization.

What results is a culture in which people feel they have license to express their inclinations to a large degree, whatever those inclinations might be. Such a culture is likely to be colorful, as this one is, and creative, as this one is, and constantly changing, as this one is. But if people are encouraged to express their inclinations, not everything they express is likely to prove to be conducive to social order. On the contrary, give people that license and you can count on a high measure of social disorder, even breakdown. For the particular characteristic of sensation seeking, when individuals are undiscouraged from expressing themselves in this regard, those who have a high endowment of the sensation-seeking tendency will be among the most adventurous, bold, and interesting members of the culture. However, they are also likely to be attracted to sensations and experiences that the rest of the people in the culture, those with average or low sensation seeking, find obnoxious or offensive.

Heavy metal is one such sensation-filled experience for adolescents in our time. The offensiveness of it to others only enhances its attractiveness to its adherents; one appealing feature of an experience for high-sensation seekers is that it break whatever taboos exist in the culture. Heavy metal music, and other features of the heavy metal subculture, possess this feature in abundance. No matter where the borders of cultural acceptability were set, heavy metal would certainly seek to burst beyond them, in part for the high-sensation thrill of it.

Reckless behavior also involves violating the boundaries of acceptable behavior, and it appeals to metalheads and other boys partly for this reason. As we have seen, however, heavy metal music does not seem to cause boys to be destructive or antisocial. On the contrary, it has the intriguing and surprising effect of purging the anger of boys who like it and listen to it; it *calms them down.* To understand the how and why of this it helps to return to issues of socialization. Aggressiveness, like sensation seeking, is a characteristic that can be argued to vary in strength among individuals, with some having a relatively high natural endowment of it and some relatively low. Males, in general, have more of it than females, and adolescent males more than older males; in virtually every country on which records exist, now or historically, adolescent males commit a high proportion of the aggressive acts.[16] Within adolescent males as a group, however, there is a great deal of individual variability in their aggressiveness, with some relatively high, some relatively low. We cannot know precisely what an individual's genetic propensity for aggressiveness is, but we can safely make the assumption that there is genetic variability in the endowment of this characteristic as there is for most characteristics, from nose size to musical ability.

Aggressiveness is a characteristic that particularly requires socialization. No society, even a relatively lenient one, can survive if it does not teach its children as they grow up that they may not strike another person whenever they wish, that they may not take whatever they like when they see something (or someone) they find attractive. Even in the American majority culture, although self-expression is prized over self-control, children are taught at least a minimal level of self-control over their aggressiveness. Some boys, however, may find that when they reach adolescence, and the level of their aggressiveness rises with the physiological changes of puberty, the minimal restraints they have learned as children are not sufficient. In the course of the teen years, testosterone levels for boys rise to a level *up to twenty times higher* than prior to puberty,[17] and testosterone is known to be related to aggressiveness. As a consequence many boys feel intense aggressiveness. Yet they know it is not socially acceptable to express aggressiveness by harming another person or by destroying property (although they sometimes do express it this way), and they feel their aggressiveness bursting the flimsy shackles that had been placed on it in the course of their childhood socialization. They lack the capacity for *self-regulation.*[18] What can they do? They need something to ease that aggressiveness, drain it off, lance it, *purge* it—and many of them find just this purgative in heavy metal music.

Ironically, the aggressive, antisocial anthems of heavy metal music become the palliative that spares them and those around them from the full expression of their aggressive, antisocial inclinations. Living in a culture in which the implements provided to them to quell their aggressiveness prove too meager when their aggressiveness surges in adolescence, they look to something to aid them, something outside of themselves to supplement their insufficient internal resources. They find it in heavy metal music.

Lew

Lew was the only avowed satanist in the study. Virtually all of the boys in the study laughed off the suggestion that heavy metal pro- moted satanism. They recognized some satanist elements in some of the lyrics of some bands, but they saw this as a ploy on the part of these bands to draw attention to themselves by shocking and outraging people. For Lew, however, his preference for heavy metal music was one extension of his belief in satanism, in partic- ular his belief in the occult and the power of black magic.

It was immediately evident, upon looking at him, that he was an unusual boy. His long reddish-blond hair extended three inches past his shoulders, very straight, and most of the time hung in front of his face like a reed curtain. That curtain rarely parted; in the course of an interview of over an hour, he did not allow eye contact more than once or twice, and briefly. His rare laugh was muted and languid, as if it started from somewhere deep inside of him and had nearly expired by the time it reached his mouth.

His features were very fair. Although he was sixteen years old, he had an oddly prepubescent face, with only isolated facial hairs; apparently he had never shaved. He wore the black t-shirt popu- lar among metalheads, with a heavy metal logo on it, this one pro- claiming the band King Diamond and portraying a demonic-look- ing woman. His denim jacket had the same logo and the same woman on it. He had on black pants and pointed, ankle-high, black leather shoes.

He seemed to live an isolated life, dwelling in a deep well of alienation. The black magic rituals he conducted were always soli- tary. He went alone to concerts, which generally are attended by groups of friends. "I just usually go by myself and then I meet somebody there," he said. "I see people I recognize from previous concerts, and they recognize me. I'm always the guy with the King Diamond t-shirt on."

Concerts provided these tenuous and transient social contacts for him, and they also gave him a chance to enjoy slamdancing and stagediving. Stagedivers climb onto the band's stage at a concert and then leap off into the dense crowd below; the act demands trust in the swaying mass below to soften the landing. In Lew's stagediving there were elements of sensation seeking, in that he seemed to be doing it for the excitement. It also may have had elements of a manhood test for him, a way to demonstrate his courage and fortitude.

> *I stagedive a lot. The security guards are brutal [if they catch you]. They just beat the crap out of you. [When I stagedived at a recent concert] one of them grabbed me by the foot and kind of kicked me in the face. Threatened my life. [At another concert] I jumped off the balcony [into the crowd]. [How far down?] About eleven feet. [Were people waiting to catch you?] Well, I was jumping into the crowd, but the crowd was moshing, so they were moving around. [They moved apart at the wrong time and] I kind of hit at the wrong angle. My knees swelled up like balloons.*

Stagediving can be hazardous. (Photo by Nick Romanenko)

He named as favorite songs "Die by My Hand" by Coronary (the title of the song and of the band speak for themselves) and "Melissa" by King Diamond, which is about a gory murder. King Diamond, his favorite heavy metal band, is known for the satanist themes running through their songs. But Lew's own satanism, he said, was not something intended to be evil or harmful.

It's not like anything people have ever heard. It's like—you know, you have your Christianity and things like that. It's just like a different belief, a different power. I'm into the occult, black magic. [What does that involve?] *Just private rituals. Meditation, transchanneling, automatic writing—things like that. You just kind of channel your energy source—demons, if you will.* [Do you use black magic to affect others?] *Not really. Really more focusing on yourself. Sure, if somebody does something [bad to you] it says strike them back a hundred fold, but I don't really get into that, because what does revenge do for somebody? It seems to me, not much.*

Why does a boy become a satanist? For Lew, it was certainly not because his parents taught him those beliefs; he described his mother as being "kind of religious," in the Christian, not satanist, sense. Yet his beliefs did appear to be at least partly rooted in his family life, in particular his anguish over his parents' divorce when he was eleven years old and years of conflict before that time. When his mother and father first separated, the anguish of it triggered what Lew believed was his first contact with the dead, in particular a sense of the presence of his grandmother, who had died when he was two years old. He had found her presence consoling, and it had led him to occult practices that would provide a more systematic way of trying to contact her again.

The episode involving his grandmother may be understood as a child's desperate search for consolation under intolerably painful conditions. However, some of his more recent experiences with spirits were more worrisome, more suggestive of psychological disturbance—although he rejected that interpretation. He spoke cryptically of demonic forces active in himself, shiny shapes and voices.

[What makes you think they're demonic?] *Through automatic writing.* [Demons write through you?] *Yeah, they could. Yeah.* [What sort of things?] *Some stuff you just can't read. And some stuff could be in other languages. You just really don't know. It's really strange. You can see where it's writing, but you're not moving your hands [intentionally].* [Have you showed the automatic writing to anybody?] *Yeah. People from school. They have this counseling guy. I showed it to him.* [What did he think?] *He thought it was crazy. He said, "It's really your unconscious." I said, "Yeah." You know, people try to rationalize everything. There's just some things that the human mind cannot comprehend.*

Lew's alienation was perhaps the deepest of any of the boys in the study, so deep it was almost appalling. Other metalheads, although they might be estranged from family, community, school, and religion, at least had friends who were important to them, and Lew did not. I listened to him and thought to myself, This is a kid whose culture has utterly failed to provide him with anything to structure his life around. Someone might retort, "Well, it's up to him to find that." But that is precisely the point: In the contemporary West we leave it up to individuals to find their own sources of meaning, rather than socializing them into meaningful group identities of family, clan, religion, and so on. Left on his own in this way, Lew gravitated to the bizarre, grotesque world of satanism and a spirit world of demons. I wondered, and worried, what would become of a boy like Lew, in the long run. But when he spoke of what he might be doing in ten years, there seemed to be some possibility of hope in his future. At least he was original.

[What do you see yourself doing in ten years?] *Probably playing in clubs in a heavy metal band. I'm a singer, and I've sung with a couple of [heavy metal] groups. I write all the music, too. I'd like to go to a [music] conservatory in London and learn from the big opera guys. I really like opera and musical theater. So I'd like to combine opera and heavy metal. It'd have a horror basis; it would be a horror-opera.*

Summary profile: Lew

Age: 16
Race: White
Education: currently in 10th grade

Father's occupation: hospital worker
Mother's occupation: homemaker
Family background: parents divorced five years ago
Number of heavy metal recordings owned: about 250
Favorite heavy metal groups: King Diamond, Metalchurch, Iron Maiden, Slayer
Goals in ten years: play in clubs with heavy metal band, write "horror-operas" combining opera and heavy metal
Political orientation: liberal Democrat
Religious orientation: occult, black magic, satanism
Hobbies/leisure preferences: plays guitar, collects comic books, lifts weights, jogs
Three people most admired: Andrew Lloyd Webber, Stephen King, Edgar Allan Poe
Number of times in past year:

Driven a car under the influence of alcohol:	0
Driven a car over 80 miles per hour:	0
Driven a car greater than 20 mph over speed limit:	0
Had sex without contraception:	>10
Had sex with someone not known well:	6–10
Used marijuana:	2–5
Used cocaine:	0
Used illegal drugs other than marijuana or cocaine:	0
Damaged or destroyed public or private property:	2–5
Shoplifted:	0

Sources of Alienation I:
Family and Community

The family's importance in our society [has] been steadily declining over a period of more than 100 years. [The result, in the present, is that children learn] a certain protective shallowness, a fear of binding commitments, a willingness to pull up roots whenever the need arises, a dislike of depending on anyone, an incapacity for loyalty or gratitude.

—**Christopher Lasch, *Haven in a Heartless World***

In our society, the forces that produce youthful alienation are growing in strength and scope. Families, schools, and other institutions that play important roles in human development are rapidly being eroded.

—**Urie Bronfenbrenner, professor emeritus of human development, Cornell University**

As we have seen, the dominant theme in heavy metal songs is alienation, alienation with respect to personal relationships as well as social institutions. Violence is pervasive in the songs, and the violence expresses a deep alienation, a sense of being at war with the world. Songs about lovers—or former lovers—bemoan their faithlessness and duplicity. Songs about politics and religion are invariably cynical: All politicians are liars and schemers, all religious figures are hypocrites. The singer is presented as a lone figure of integrity trying to hold out against a massive tide of corruption and ugliness. Little hope is offered for turning that tide, for ridding the world of its multiple ills and creating a society free of the ugliness of the present one. The best that can be hoped for, it seems, is to go down nobly, to be the rare voice crying in the wilderness, even with the certainty that the world at large will never listen.

Given the pervasiveness of the theme of alienation in heavy metal music, it will come as no surprise that many of the adolescents who like heavy metal are unhappy with their family relationships, express negative attitudes toward school, and tend to be cynical about politics and re-

Much of adolescents' time at home is spent alone in their rooms; this is true of heavy metal fans and many other adolescents as well. (Photo by Nick Romanenko)

ligion. There are exceptions, of course. Nevertheless, the alienation that is characteristic of metalheads in general is striking, disturbing, and worth exploring.

I have raised the question, How did it happen that such a cynical and alienated ideology as heavy metal has gained such a large and devoted following among adolescents? Part of the answer seems to be that the lack of faith among these adolescents in the reliability and meaning of their social ties is based on the real deterioration of these ties over the past two centuries. As a consequence of this deterioration, many adolescents growing up today find themselves without the bonds to family, community, and religion that most people have taken for granted in most times and in most cultures. Where *family* is concerned, it is clear that the reason many of them are reluctant to rely much on family ties is that they have learned, from hard and bitter experience, that such ties cannot be trusted—parents often divorce, typically after years of vicious domestic battles. Where ties to *community* and *friends* are concerned, the mobility typical of American families makes these ties tentative and transitory in each new place, for many boys. Where *school* is concerned, many of them describe their experiences with loathing and their teachers as adversaries. Where *religion* is concerned, these adolescents have learned the tolerance of Western liberalism so well that it has made them not just accepting of the right of individuals to believe whatever they please, but doubtful that any creed contains any reliable truth. In this chapter metalheads' ties to family and community will be described and discussed; in Chapter 7 we will explore ties to school, religion, and friends.

Socialization in the family

Before describing the particular characteristics of the families of the boys in the study, some general remarks are warranted concerning parents and socialization. In considering the attitudes and behavior of parents, it is important to recognize at the outset that what parents do is influenced by the larger culture in which the family lives; to a large extent their parenting reflects their culture. To put it in the terms of the socialization theory introduced in Chapter 2, the socialization that occurs in the family is heavily influenced by the characteristics of the cultural belief system. No parent chooses parenting practices *ex nihilo*; all parents have learned from their culture certain guidelines for what kind of person they should expect their child to become, and also what their response should be when a child defies parental expectations. The guidelines parents learn have an ideological basis; implicitly, by acting in certain ways in their role as parents, parents declare what they believe parents should do in relation to children and what characteristics they are seeking to nourish and promote in their children. The key issue in this respect is whether parents, following their culture, consider it more important to promote the obedience and conformity characteristic of narrow socialization, on the one hand, or the individualism and self-expression of broad socialization, on the other.

As described in Chapter 2, the belief system held by parents in the majority culture of the United States, from which virtually all of the metalheads in this study come, is characterized by broad socialization values in which individualism and self-expression take precedence well above obedience and conformity.[1] Parents in the United States generally believe that the focus of their childrearing should be on promoting these values in their children. This means demanding as little obedience as possible, in order to allow the child's natural inclinations to develop and find expression. The idea that parents should insist that their children treat them with deference and obey their wishes—even when the children have grown into adolescence and then adulthood—would strike most parents in the American middle class as oppressive and unhealthy. The motto of American parents in the majority culture is to do everything possible to help their child become an independent individual.

Parents of Metalheads: Pals and Adversaries

Among the boys in this study, one result of this broad socialization approach to parenting seems to be that many boys see their parents not as people who exercise authority over them and to whom they owe obedience but rather as friends, confidants, near-equals.[2] "They're my best friends," Scott said of his parents. "They're real down-to-our-level parents." Bill described his parents as "good friends you can talk to." Not only do the boys not see their parents as having legitimate authority over them, the parents themselves do not see such authority as part of their role, at least in some cases. Erik said that his parents "are like really intelligent and mature about everything, so they've never really disapproved of anything if I've wanted to do it." Henry praised his parents for the freedom of choice and activity they had always allowed him:

> They've been extremely tolerant of whatever pursuit that I decided to go into. They've always respected my opinion, since I was real small. I can go up to my dad and say, "Hey, Bob, what's up?" and just talk to him as a friend. [You call him by his first name?] Yeah. I've always had that relationship with my parents. [Your mom, too?] No, my mom, I call her "Shorty." She's real small.

Nor is this free rein necessarily something that is initiated in adolescence, in recognition of the child's increasing maturity and competence. Mike said he had liked heavy metal music since he was four years old. He had taken a liking to it from hearing his parents play it around the house. "I went to nursery school one day when I was four, with the Black Sabbath *Master of Reality* album," he recalled. "And they called my parents; they thought something was wrong with me. And my parents were, like, 'That's what he listens to.' It was pretty funny."

One sometimes gets a sense, from the interviews, of parents who are unsure about the extent and the limits of their authority, afraid of seeming insufficiently tolerant in their own eyes or those of their children, and uncertain about whether their authority would be respected if they did try to exercise it. Ben's parents had expressed concern over his interest in heavy metal, but with some diffidence:

> They basically trust my judgment and don't worry about it. My dad a couple of times had talks with me, saying he knows I have good judgment and so forth, but that he thinks some of the lyrics do get out of hand. And they were very brief talks. I just said, "Look, Dad, don't worry about it," and he left me alone.

Mark's mother, like many of the parents, did not allow her own revulsion at heavy metal themes to extend to parenting practices that would restrict the expression of his interest in metal. "She thinks the Iron Maiden posters I have in my room are disgusting, but she doesn't want me to take them down. She's always, like, 'Whatever you want to do, that's fine with me. It's your life. You live it the way you want to.'"

The evident suspicion on the part of the parents, that their authority would not be respected by their children if they tried to exercise it, is not unfounded. Parents who did try to restrict the extent to which their boys listened to heavy metal met with little success. Neil easily brushed off his mother's attempts to influence his music listening, even to the mild degree of attempting to get him to play it not quite so loud. "My mom says, 'Why do you have to play it loud?' And I go, 'Well, metal's supposed to be played loud.' [*Does she ever prohibit you from playing it loud?*] No, she just complains about it. There's nothing she can do. I just say, 'Tough, Mom.'" Matt's mother was one of only two parents of boys in the study who actually went to the extent of confiscating her boy's heavy metal recordings, but she also met with little respect or success in her efforts. "She doesn't like [heavy metal], but she has to put up with it," said Matt. "She's tried taking away all my tapes, and I've lost a lot of tapes that way. I've gotten to where I hide them. I've got me one of those big tool boxes, with a lock on it."

The boys' defiance and the impotence of their parents' authority is not restricted only to heavy metal. "My dad bitches a lot, but I can handle him," said Rich with blasé assurance. He gave an example of his father attempting to get him to mow the lawn, and how he had to ask Rich over and over again. "I just start laughing at him. [*What does he do when you laugh at him?*] He just gets more pissed off. And then I laugh even harder. I end up doing what he asked me to do, but usually he tells me three or four times before I get up and do it."

Alienation and Divorce; Divorce and Family Conflict

All three of the boys just described—Neil, Matt, and Rich—have parents who are divorced. Divorce makes it all the more difficult for parents to exercise credible authority over their children. When Rich's father asks him to mow the lawn, Rich can ignore him or laugh at him with the knowledge that no matter how angry his father becomes, they are together only for the weekend and see each other only every other weekend. It is easy to imagine, too, how defiance by an adolescent boy might be a way of expressing his resentment at his father for leaving the home, and how guilt on the part of a father over the divorce would make him all the more reluctant to enforce compliance. For a mother, the absence of the father removes from the home a crucial ally and makes it more difficult for her to require compliance from her adolescent boy, who is growing bigger and stronger daily in the course of his teens. Add to this the increased burdens of household work, employment, and economic privation that typically fall on mothers in the aftermath of a divorce, and it is not surprising that they might find it difficult to summon consistently the time and energy involved in parenting an adolescent boy.[3]

Thirty-six percent of the metalheads in the study were from divorced families. This is significantly higher than the percentage among the boys in the comparison group (22 percent), and the rates in both groups are a testimony to the pervasiveness of divorce among the families of children growing up today. From the metalheads' descriptions of their family lives, it is evident that witnessing family conflict and divorce has contributed to their alienation and cynicism. This alienation and cynicism has culminated, for some, in a radical individualism, a belief that they are left to their own resources in this world, for better or worse. This is reflected in Lew's description of his parents' divorce, which took place about five years ago when he was eleven years old. "It was really confusing because one side tells you one thing and the other side tells you another," he said. "You don't know who to believe. That's where I finally developed trust in myself. People are good, but not all people are reliable. It's sad to say, but it's just a fact of life." Overall, boys from divorced families reported significantly worse family relationships than boys in nondivorced families, on the scale from which the items in Table 6.1 are taken. This pattern was true for metalheads taken alone, nonmetalheads taken alone, and for the two groups combined.

Some divorced parents remarry, of course, but this may only add to the alienation and resentment that already exist from the divorce. I do not mean to imply that this is inevitably the case—certainly there are many stepparents and stepchildren who have excellent relationships—only that the resentments and divided loyalties sometimes characteristic of stepfamily life can be a source of adolescent alienation. It is worth noting that conflicts between remarried couples most often concern their children from the previous marriages, and also that relationships between stepparents and stepchildren are often high in conflict.[4] This is displayed in the lives of some of the metalheads. Recall the incident described in Mark's profile preceding Chapter 3, where he and his stepfather had a disagreement over which TV program to watch. It ended with his stepfather slapping him and Mark retaliating by punching his stepfather in the face and jumping on his back, breaking his nose and his knee and fracturing his skull.

Remarrying parents sometimes bring children into the new marriage, who become stepsiblings for the children of their new spouse and another potential source of alienation and resentment for all the children involved. This is not always true, of course; no doubt there are many stepfamilies where stepsiblings find in each other good friends and companions. But in exploring the various sources responsible for the anger and alienation characteristic of the metalheads, it is evident that conflict in a stepfamily may be one such source. Boys who have been troublesome to their parents before the divorce may find themselves subject to unflattering comparisons to more compliant stepsiblings and not the least bit happy with their stepsiblings for providing the contrast. "My stepbrother, man, he's the biggest brownnoser in the world," said Matt contemptuously. "Kisses up to my dad, kisses up to his mom. He turned off my [heavy metal] music one day, and I almost busted him. I'm against everything he is."

Nick, whose profile precedes Chapter 2, has never had a good relationship with his father. An alcoholic, his father beat him regularly the whole time Nick was growing up, a pattern that ended only after an altercation in which Nick, by then seventeen and muscular, "picked him up and body-slammed him on the cement." Since then (Nick is now twenty-three), his father has never dared strike him. But Nick is bewildered and angry that his father, after treating Nick so badly for all these years, treats his new stepson much differently:

For a while I had to live with my dad and his wife and her two children. And her son, my dad buys him computers and gets him all kinds of shit, and is putting him through college. Yet he refused to pay for me to go to art school. He just figured I'd be a failure. He said it was too competitive and he didn't think I could make the grades. I don't think I can ever forgive him for that, that he didn't have any faith and he figured I would be a failure.

Although these examples (and abundant evidence from other studies) indicate that parents' divorce and remarriage can have troubling effects on children, most of the parents of the metalheads are not divorced and many of the parents of nonmetalheads *are* divorced, which suggests that divorce by itself is not something that necessarily leads either to alienation or to an attraction to heavy metal music. Studies over the past two decades on the effects of divorce on children indicate that it may not be divorce alone that promotes alienation, but the family conflict and unhappy family relationships that are typically a part of divorce.[5] Divorce is often a reflection and an outcome of these problems, but they can exist in nondivorced families as well.

Whatever the cause, it is clear that metalheads' experience in their families tends to be unhappier, compared to other boys. Table 6.1 compares the boys on items from a questionnaire about family relationships.[6] The metalheads have a more negative view of their family lives on every item, but a few items particularly stand out. One is that nearly half of the metalheads (43 percent) agree with the statement "I try to stay away from home most of the time," compared to only 20 percent of the other boys. This indicates that many of the metalheads do not feel comfortable or welcome at home. Another striking difference is on their responses to the item, "When I grow up and have a family, it will be in at least a few ways similar to my own." Eighty-seven percent of nonmetalheads but only 66 percent of the metalheads agreed with this statement. This indicates that many of the metalheads see their family lives as unhappy and have no intention of emulating (even in "a few ways") the kind of family life their parents have created for them.

TABLE 6.1   Attitudes Toward Family

	Percent Responding "Yes"	
Item	Metalheads	Others
I try to stay away from home most of the time.	43	20
When I grow up and have a family, it will be in at least a few ways similar to my own.	66	87
When my parents are strict, I feel that they are right, even if I get angry.	51	70
Most of the time my parents get along well with each other.	67	88
My parents are ashamed of me.	16	3
I have been carrying a grudge against my parents for years.	20	8
My parents are divorced.	36	22

Family Socialization in Cultural Context

Of course, family life can be problematic and alienating not only for adolescents, but for their parents as well. Numerous studies indicate that parent-child conflict is highest when children are in adolescence, and parents' enjoyment of their role as parents is lowest during this time. One reason for this is the absence or tenuousness of ecological connections between family and neighborhood, family and school, family and community, family and religious organizations.[7] For most families in the American majority culture, these connections are either nonexistent or too loose to have an important role in confirming and buttressing family efforts at socialization. Peers and media, meanwhile, often actively subvert family control. Adolescents spend more time with their friends than they do with their families,[8] and illegal and antisocial activities such as alcohol and drug use and vandalism tend to take place with friends, in groups.[9] The media tend to promote immediate gratification and self-indulgence (particularly through advertising), which acts to subvert the socialization goal of self-regulation.[10] Thus American parents face a daunting task when their children reach adolescence, and they face it alone.

To get a better sense of the predicament of parents in the contemporary United States, consider a contrast with a more traditional community. Among the Sambia of New Guinea, boys traditionally spend their first seven years of life mostly in the company of their mother and other women and their children.[11] At age seven they are removed from their mothers' care and live from that age until manhood in the company of men and other boys, learning the skills that will enable them to be economically successful as adults as well as the cultural beliefs that are part of the Sambian heritage. In this village as in other traditional communities, it is not the nuclear family alone that participates in the socialization of a boy. The adults in the extended family—grandmothers, aunts, older siblings, and cousins in early childhood, grandfathers and uncles after age seven—are part of the child's everyday life and have authority over him similar to that of the parents. People in the surrounding neighborhood and community know the child and keep track of him, in the sense of expressing care and goodwill for him as well as in the sense of criticizing him for behavior that is antisocial or otherwise unacceptable, behavior that reflects either a lack of self-regulation or a failure to comply with community norms. The family shares with the community an adherence to the Sambian belief system, which sets clear standards of what is right and wrong, good and bad, venerable and contemptible. These standards in turn set implicitly the intended outcome of socialization: to shape a child into an adult who behaves in ways that are right, good, and venerable. In such an environment we might say that socialization is *integrated,* from family to neighborhood and community to the cultural belief system, which gives coherence to the socialization pattern of the culture as a whole. All elements work to promote the same ends in the socialization of the children.

The degree of integration in the socialization that takes place in the majority culture of the United States is obviously much lower, and the reasons for that are many, including a long American tradition of independent family life, as well as the advanced technological status of the present American economy that makes children's obedience less crucial to sheer survival than in a preindustrial economy. Regardless of the reasons, however, the consequences are that parents are largely left on their own in the socialization of their children and receive little direct support, even from their closest relatives.

Alienation and the Missing Extended Family

In the majority culture of the United States few adolescents live within even 100 miles of their nearest grandparent.[12] Living so far away, most children are lucky to see their grandparents even once or twice a year.[13] As a consequence, grandparents are generally not available to provide nurturance at times when parents are too busy or too preoccupied with their own problems to provide it themselves. Grandparents are not available to provide solace and refuge to children whose parents are fighting or divorcing or who, for one reason or another, have rejected or neglected their children. Again, there are many, many exceptions to this, and many adolescents, including many metalheads, have grandparents who live close by and with whom they have close relationships. But for those who do not, this may be another contributor to their sense of isolation and alienation.

This was expressed most poignantly by two boys, Reggie and Lew. In both cases, the emotional vacuum at the heart of their family lives had led them to magnify the emotional significance of tenuous long-distance contacts with their grandparents. Reggie's parents are divorced and he lives with his mother, but mother and son are so estranged that they barely speak to each other:

> It's gotten to the point where we just communicate by notes in the kitchen on the refrigerator. By the time I get up in the summertime she's already gone to work, and by the time she gets home I've already gone out. We can't have a conversation and not have an argument.

He has rarely seen his father since the divorce four years ago, and he has no brothers or sisters. The one family tie he values is to his grandparents—but they live in England, and he sees them only once every few years for a brief visit. Nevertheless, he cherishes and nurtures that tie: "They have a very high opinion of me. That's one family relationship I'd like to keep intact, long-distance as it may be." Even though he sees them so rarely, it comforts and sustains him to know the tie is there. "I love them, they love me, that's enough." There is something faintly pathetic about it, something desperate about his emotional reliance on these distant figures while the family relationships in close proximity lie shattered and ruined around him. But it is all he has in the way of family ties, and it is better than nothing.

Lew's ties to his grandparents, specifically his grandmother, stretch across an even greater distance—the divide between life and death. As described earlier, his parents divorced when he was eleven, and the disillusionment and confusion of it was so great that he no longer trusts either of them. Like Reggie, he was left with only a relationship to a grandparent to rely upon for nurturance. However, in Lew's case his grandmother, the only grandparent he knew, died when he was just two years old. Nevertheless it was from her that he drew comfort at the deepest crisis during his parents divorce:

> When my parents first divorced, there was a lot of stress and confusion, and in a young child that can also release a lot of spiritual energy, I think. And so I was crying and everything the first night my mom took me and we left, and I got up to go to the bathroom and I thought I heard something. I remembered that she always used to give me vanilla wafers and milk, and there was a strong smell of vanilla wafers and milk. So I went into the kitchen, but there was nothing in there. But there were some stairs there [leading into the cellar], and when I looked there I kind of saw a light, and I could hear her talking. She was just telling me not to be afraid and everything would work out and you have to piece your life together and go on.

It was this experience that eventually led him to satanism, in particular black magic, in order to learn rituals that would enable him to contact his grandmother again in the next world.

Alienation and the community: The role of geographical mobility

Another important aspect of the isolation of families is the absence of ties between family and community. One of the primary reasons for this is the high level of geographical mobility that characterizes contemporary American society.[14] It is easy to see the influence of this mobility on the lives of the metalheads, on their families, and on their socialization. Moving has often been disruptive to their family lives, and it interferes with the development of an attachment to a particular neighborhood and community. Certainly not all children react with unhappiness and anger when their families move from place to place every few years. Depending on their temperament, on their adaptability to new situations, some may find it exciting and fun to move to a new place, make new friends, experience a different environment.[15] Others, however, are left weary and wary from repeatedly making social ties to friends, classmates, teachers, and neighbors, only to have to break those ties yet again. They may become reluctant to make close ties in a new place, unwilling to open themselves up to the pain of cutting those ties when their families move again.

I was not expecting to find this in the interviews, and I did not ask about it in a systematic way. For this reason it is difficult to say how many of the boys felt this way about moving, nor can I say how the metalheads compare in this respect to other boys. But let me offer a couple of examples, which illustrate the effect that high mobility *can* have on boys. I think the examples indicate that at least for some boys, high mobility can contribute to their alienation and cynicism. This seemed clear in Ben's case:

> My dad worked for Coca-Cola, and we've lived [in] so many places. We've lived—oh, God—everywhere, it seems like. Hong Kong, Philippines, Greece . . . once we got back here from Hong Kong, I had it dead set in my mind that I was not gonna make any more friends. No more. 'Cause every time I make a friend I lose him. We always move. It's just not worth doing it anymore.

Now that he has been living in Atlanta for over a year, he has begun to open up somewhat and make friends. "I realized I was going to be here a little bit longer," he said. Still, the impression left by his family's high mobility is clear.

Derek's situation was different from Ben's. Rather than moving repeatedly every few years as Ben's family did, Derek's family moved only once, but at a crucial time: just as he was about to enter his senior year of high school. Like Ben, he reacted with pain and bitterness at first, although he eventually learned to accommodate himself to his new home.

> The kids I grew up with from kindergarten, I went to school with them all the way through eleventh grade. And then I had to move, which really destroyed me, the fact that I couldn't graduate with all those kids. At first I came to my school, like, "I'm not going to talk to anybody." But then I said, "Well, I might as well make the best of it." And I ended up making a lot of friends.

Heavy metal as a consolation for alienation in the family

Overall, then, it is evident that the family ties of many of the boys are tenuous, frayed, damaged, or nonexistent. Even in the stable families, parents rarely see it as part of their role to restrict, inhibit, or discipline their adolescent children. This is not (in most cases) because they do not care about their children but because they are part of a culture that values individualism and self-expression very highly, self-restraint and self-denial very little. Parents have imbibed this belief system from their culture, and they believe they are doing the best thing for their children when they allow them free rein and look the other way when their children are doing things they find morally objectionable.

In addition, the family lives of many of these boys are *not* stable, but have been subjected to periods of intense conflict, often including divorce and sometimes remarriage. For many boys these have been bitter experiences that have led them to despise one parent or the other and have made them disillusioned with both. The disillusionment extends beyond family relationships to a general mistrust of emotional ties, a reluctance to place much faith in anyone—except oneself. Thus the individualism characteristic of the metalheads derives not only from a culture that exalts individualism and parents who promote it because they live in that culture and represent it to their children. It also extends from the metalheads' own experience—that ties to others cannot be relied upon, that trusting others can be severely painful, that ultimately the only person you can trust to be around when you need them is *you*. The high mobility of American society also contributes to this: It is dangerous to develop close ties to a community (friends, neighbors, schoolteachers) because when you leave the pain will be hard to bear.

The result is that the boys are not an integrated part of a family that is in turn part of a community that is in turn part of a society—the way virtually all children in virtually all cultures have grown up historically—but atoms who are drifting through social space on their own, occasionally bumping transiently against other atoms, slamdancing their way through life. Mark's description of how he lives with his mother and stepfather is extreme but emblematic. The house they live in together is divided into two parts:

> I just stay in my half and they stay in their half. There's a door dividing the two. What usually happens is, I'll come home from work and I'll watch TV until about six or six-thirty. That's about the time their dinner's over. And then I'll leave the living room and go to my room and stay there for the remainder of the night and they'll stay in the living room by themselves watching TV.

This dire portrait is not true of all metalheads' family relationships. There is diversity in this as in all of their characteristics, and some of the boys had healthy and loving relationships with their parents.[16] But if we are seeking to understand the appeal of heavy metal for adolescent boys and the reasons why lyrical themes of alienation and nihilism should appeal to them, the nature of their family lives provides important clues. For many of them the alienation in the lyrical themes speaks to the pervasive alienation they experience in their own family relationships. They did not need to listen to Metallica's "And Justice for All" or Iron Maiden's "Be Quick or Be Dead" in order to learn that the adult world is rife with deceit and betrayal; they know it already from their own experience, and when they hear it in a song they seize the message, their hearts resonate to it, and they are ready to raise their fists and bang their heads in sympathy. They did not need to hear Megadeth's "In My Darkest Hour" to realize that they have been left on their own in the world, and that if they plan to make anything of their lives or find any happiness they had better be prepared to do it themselves, as lonely and defiant individuals, because no one is going to provide the answers or even offer help in finding answers. They would know all this whether or not they had ever listened to heavy metal songs. But heavy metal songs provide them with an expression of their anger and angst, of which their fragmented family relationships are an important source, and give them the comfort of knowing that they are not the only ones who are suffering. There is something consoling in the bond they feel to others through the music, even if the bond is based on a shared sense of isolation and alienation.

Durkheim speaks, from a distance of nearly a century ago, as if he had attended a recent heavy metal concert:

> The more the family and community become foreign to the individual, so much the more does he become a mystery to himself, unable to escape the exasperating and agonizing question: to what purpose? . . . For individuals share too deeply in the life of society for it to be diseased without their suffering infection. . . . Then new moralities originate which, by elevating facts to ethics, commend suicide or at least tend in that direction by suggesting a minimal existence. On their appearance they seem to have been created out of whole cloth by their makers who are sometimes blamed for the pessimism of their doctrines. In reality they are an effect rather than a cause; they merely symbolize the physiological distress of the body social. [They do not cause the individual to be alienated, but simply] drive him more vigorously on the way to which he is already inclined by the state of moral distress directly aroused in him by the disintegration of society. [But] however individualized a man may be, there is always something collective remaining—the very depression and melancholy resulting from this same exaggerated individualism. He effects communion through sadness when he no longer has anything else with which to achieve it.[17]

Reggie

In his appearance, Reggie was not a typical metalhead. A handsome young black man, he had short, simply styled hair and was nicely dressed in a loose blue denim shirt and fashionable black-and-white pants, although he wore no shoes (it was, after all, a July day in Atlanta). A senior in high school, he was exceptionally articulate for his age and also humorous, in a sardonic way. Although he did not look the part, he was a devoted metalhead. He had a job writing about popular music for a local teen magazine, which he felt gave him a certain authority to debunk misconceptions about heavy metal music.

A lot of people say it's garbage, it's loud, everything sounds the same, it's just people screaming. I say that if you really listen to it, if you know what you're talking about and you really read the lyrics, you wouldn't say that. I consider myself to be a student of it, you know what I mean? 'Cause I work for this magazine, and I've interviewed basically every [metal] band that's come to Atlanta for the past four-and-a-half, five years.

He was skeptical of the idea that heavy metal music should be blamed for human violence and venality. Nasty and violent acts take place every day, he pointed out, and few of the people committing them listen to heavy metal. He also rejected the claim that heavy metal music contributes to suicide. To him, the music was being made a scapegoat for the real problems that teenagers have that drive some of them to suicide.

As far as this thing about teen suicide, if a kid's really disturbed and if his parents aren't bright enough or don't care enough to pick up on it, then it's partly their responsibility, too. What's so funny is that if a kid's listening to a heavy metal record and he kills himself, they blame it on the music. But, you're telling me, with the suicide rate the way it is for teenagers in this country, that all these kids listen to heavy metal?

111

Although he was in no way depressed or suicidal himself, he had his own share of problems. His parents were divorced and he was alienated from both of them. He lived with his mother, but they avoided each other to the point where they communicated through notes on the refrigerator. "We don't agree on anything, religion-wise, politically, or what I should do with my life," he said. His mother disliked heavy metal and suspected that it had a bad effect on him.

She thinks that underneath I'm like a Charles Manson, like a psychopath. She says, "You're into all this weird stuff." [Does she mean the music?] *Yeah. She's like, "You're a blockhead. Turn that shit off! I've been at work all day, I don't want to hear it." She thinks I should be listening to rap.*

He saw himself as resisting his mother's attempts to make him conform to the middle-class norm. He wanted something more unusual, more exciting than that.

What I'd like to do is be a music critic for a heavy metal magazine or some other kind of music magazine. I'm not the kind of person that can get a nine-to-five job or do something I hated—that's not me. And my mom, she thinks I should have a structured kind of life, and I'm not a structured kind of person. [Structured in what sense?] *That I should get up Monday through Friday, go to my same job, come home, watch TV, and go to bed. Maybe on the weekends go to a football game.* [You don't want the average American middle-class lifestyle?] *No, because I'm not an average person.*

His relations with his father were similarly tense.

[How often do you see your dad?] *About every two weeks.* [Do you get along better with him than with your mother?] *No. Otherwise I'd live with him. My dad's English, to begin with. And Catholic. And whereas I believe in abortion, he does not, and that's just ugly, period.*

The music had had a powerful, ineffable attraction for him since the time he was quite young, nine years old. He heard his parents play Motown music as he was growing up, but none of it gripped him, none of it excited him, the way heavy metal did.

From the first time I heard it on the radio, it was the only music I ever really listened to. I listened to my mom's James Brown and Aretha Franklin records, the Supremes and all that, I heard that around the house a lot growing up, but I never really connected with it. [What was it about heavy metal music that you liked so much?] *That's what's so weird—I can't tell you. I could give you all this information about heavy metal, but I cannot tell you why I'm so attracted to it. I can say, "it's exciting, it gets me off," which is all true, but I can't really tell you why.*

Although it was hard for him to describe the appeal of heavy metal beyond the fact that he found it exciting, it was evident that the pessimism and the social consciousness of the lyrical themes of the songs appealed to him. Heavy metal songs spoke his own feelings about the bleak state of the world. "If you read the lyrics of any Metallica album, they're incredible, they're so intelligent." *[Most of the topics are pretty gloomy.]* "Well, this world is gloomy. I mean, there's a lot of bad things going on." He had strong opinions on religion and politics, and he expressed those opinions with complexity and detail, along with flashes of his sardonic wit.

On religion:

I don't believe in religion, period. Even if I said I'm a Christian and I prayed and I went to church with my parents, if there is God up there He knows I don't believe. I'd still be going to hell, according to what they teach. I don't believe in a god. I don't. You cannot go beyond outer space, period. Maybe it's just beyond my way of thinking and my little human mind and I'm young and stupid, but I just can't see it happening. I'm sorry. I can't see me burning in some eternal pit of fire with some dude with a pitchfork and a tail sticking out of his ass, I'm sorry. . . . I know a lot about every general religion. I believe I should educate myself before I make my decision. But still, I just don't believe it.

On politics:

I'm a Republican. I believe economically it's a good party to be with. And they let [other countries] know that while we're striving for peace and we don't want to go to war, we're not going to back down, either. I think that's the attitude you've got to take. [Would you call yourself conservative or liberal?] *Liberal. I'm not as antigovernment as most*

Republicans. Because I believe government is [good for] certain things. If there wasn't a government there wouldn't even be this university. There would be nothing if there wasn't a government. There would be nude chaos running through the streets. In fact, there wouldn't be any streets.

Reggie was also a proponent of patriotism and the American dream. Like many of the boys, his alienation from the world and his pessimism about the future of the world did not prevent him from being optimistic about his own future. He did not see his skin color as in any way an obstacle to his ambitions. "I'm a big believer that America is a very good country," he said. "You won't hear a lot of black people say that. And I think that's so wrong because this is the only country where if you actually want something bad enough, you work for it, and you'll get it. No matter what you are."

He had, however, experienced prejudice and felt the sting of it—but for being a metalhead, not for being black.

There's still a lot of prejudice out there. A lot of people say, "God, all these heavy metal kids are so angry, they're so violent, they're so whatever." I don't like the stereotype that kids who listen to heavy metal are real stupid, we all do drugs, we're all three years behind in high school, we're all dropouts, we're all going to end up derelicts.

Ironically, however, Reggie fit very strongly the stereotype of metalheads as highly reckless adolescent boys. As his Summary Profile indicates, he was involved in high levels of reckless behavior across many areas. What would become of him, in ten or twenty years? If he survived his reckless adolescence, with his intelligence and determination perhaps he would achieve his own version of the heavy metal dream: writing books on heavy metal bands. In any case he seemed unlikely to end up doing anything very conventional. He was dedicated to being unpredictable—within limits. "I don't like being predictable, to a certain extent," he said. "I mean, I don't want to be to the point where I'm so unpredictable that I'm living on the street with nothing to eat. It's kind of uncool to be so unpredictable that you don't know if you're going to eat or not."

Summary profile: Reggie

Age: 17
Race: Black
Education: in senior year of high school
Current occupation: writes on popular music for local teen magazine
Father's occupation: unknown
Mother's occupation: administrative assistant
Family background: parents divorced, high conflict with mother
Spent most of childhood in: Atlanta
Number of heavy metal recordings owned: about 80
Favorite heavy metal groups: Dirty Blonz, Skid Row, Metallica
Goals in ten years: writing books on heavy metal music or editor of a music
   magazine
Political orientation: liberal Republican
Religious orientation: atheist
Hobbies/leisure preferences: none
Number of times in past year:

Driven a car under the influence of alcohol:	>10
Driven a car over 80 miles per hour:	>50
Driven a car greater than 20 mph over speed limit:	>50
Had sex without contraception:	>10
Had sex with someone not known well:	>10
Used marijuana:	>10
Used cocaine:	6–10
Used illegal drugs other than marijuana or cocaine:	>10
Damaged or destroyed public or private property:	2–5
Shoplifted:	2–5

7

Sources of Alienation II: School and Religion

[American] schools often appear to be lonely, even harsh places, and children become increasingly disengaged from school the longer they are in attendance.

—Harold Stevenson and James Stigler, *The Learning Gap*

The crisis of society is, of course, the crisis of organized religion too: religion is no longer valid as a hero system, and so the youth scorn it.

—Ernest Becker, *The Denial of Death*

The fraying and breaking of traditional social ties experienced by many contemporary adolescents is evident not only in the family lives of the metalheads, but in other areas of their lives as well, particularly in their attitudes toward school and religion. School is an active source of alienation for many of them; they do not like it, and they resent and resist having to attend. Religion as a source of alienation is more complex. There are some who are contemptuous of it, who cite the hypocrisy of televangelists and the acquisitiveness of organized religion as evidence that all religion is a sham, but most are simply indifferent to it. It does not move them. It adds to their alienation for what it *fails* to provide for them: It does *not* give them comfort, reassurance, a stable social network outside the family, a ready source of meaning—the way it has in virtually every other society historically and cross-culturally.[1] Friends, meanwhile, are for many of them the most consistently positive source of emotional gratification in their lives.

School

Compulsory education for children is a recent historical development. It is only since the beginning of this century that Western countries have required children to attend school, and many non-Western countries still do not. The change in Western countries was based on developments in the

117

economy. As the economy became more complex, a higher level of technical skill was required to perform many of the occupations available, and
literacy became necessary for almost every occupation. At the same time,
increasing industrialization meant that children and adolescents were no
longer needed in the workforce. Entry into the workforce could be de-
layed until the midteens at least, with no harm to the economy; all the
better, in fact, since fewer adolescents would be competing with adults
for the available jobs.

Those of us who have lived all or most of our lives in the second half of
the twentieth century take it for granted that all children go to school beginning at age six or seven (increasingly, even earlier), and that most of
them continue going at least until they graduate from high school and
probably for many years beyond. However, even after the beginning of
compulsory education it took a long time before this pattern developed.
Table 7.1 shows the increase in the proportion of children enrolled in high
school and college over the course of this century.

Given the emphasis on individualism in the American cultural belief
system, American schools naturally have developed with this same emphasis. Studies of American schools describe how individualism is promoted in a variety of ways.[2] Teachers seek to enhance each child's individual abilities, rather than attempt to bring all children toward a single
standard. Rather than working mostly as a classroom or in small groups,
American students spend nearly half their time in school working alone.
Promoting children's self-esteem is considered a primary goal by both

TABLE 7.1   Educational Enrollment, 1890–1985

	Percent Enrollment, Selected Years					
	1890	*1900*	*1920*	*1940*	*1970*	*1985*
High school	6	10	30	70	90	95
College	2	4	8	16	48	57

NOTE: Figures for high school enrollment indicate percentage of 14- to 17-year-
olds in the United States in high school during the year indicated. Figures for college indicate percentage of 18- to 21-year-olds in the United States attending college during the year indicated, except for 1985, which indicates the percentage of
high school graduates that year who went on to obtain at least some college education.

SOURCES: Elder, 1987; Horowitz, 1987; U.S. Dept. of Education, 1988.

teachers and parents, so the academic work children are given varies according to their perceived ability in order to avoid the experience of failure. An individualistic rationale also underlies the practice of tracking, where children in the same grade are divided into ability groups and given different levels of materials.

This system "works," to a degree. Individual differences are indeed greater under the American system when compared to educational systems where the focus is on group rather than individual success. Also, American students tend to rate themselves as better than other children in a variety of academic tasks, suggesting that their self-esteem tends to be high. However, the costs of this system are great. Although they tend to have high opinions of their achievements, the reality is that American students rank behind students of other countries in academic achievement, especially in math achievement. In reading, a greater proportion of American students are poor readers.

Perhaps worse yet, the American emphasis on individualism has created a school environment that is experienced by students as boring and lonely, feelings that increase as they move through their school years.[3] The emphasis on individualism means not so much that they get individual attention but that they are simply expected to succeed on their own, if at all. Furthermore, much of their experience at school is passive and sedentary; there is little opportunity for them to move around, little in the way of physical activity, little that actively engages them. In one study where students were asked what in their daily lives most often makes them feel bad, school-related responses were the most frequent.[4] Other than seeing their friends, school is often experienced as a place that is "lonely and harsh," as Stevenson and Stigler put it in the epigraph that opens this chapter.

In this area as in others, the alienation of American adolescents is particularly vivid in the lives of the metalheads. Spencer had just graduated from high school, and he was glad to be rid of it.

> I hated school. It was always a living hell for me, 'cause I always saw myself as having better things to do than sit. I mean, school is valuable and you need it to a point, but once I got to about the ninth grade I figured I had learned all I was going to, and looking back I was right. I have better things to do, like practicing the guitar or reading a book or going out and getting drunk.

Rich spoke about school in the same irritated and derogatory tone:

> I didn't like school. I just didn't like it. There was nothing I liked about it. Having to do all this reading and writing, and all that stuff. I had better things to do. I didn't want to be tied down with some schoolwork that I wasn't even

going to remember in six weeks, six days. I just found it all pointless. I'd rather go out in real life and learn real-life things than sit in a classroom and read a book, answer questions from a teacher.

Many other boys shared Spencer's and Rich's pragmatic approach to school. An important part of their alienation from school is their perception that it does not provide them with information or skills that have any relevance to their present and future lives. They feel like they have "better things to do." They want to know, "What can I use this information for? And if I cannot use it for anything of practical value, what good is it?" Matt put it this way:

I think school can be almost useless 'cause teachers are just throwing stuff at you that has no purpose in life. I mean, there are some subjects that we need, but like, I'm taking English literature now and I'm not going to be writing and stuff when I grow up, so I feel that's useless.

Jack, who had dropped out of school at age sixteen, expressed similar sentiments:

The whole time I was in school I felt I was listening to a teacher teach stuff that really does not apply to any reality. Why should I be there when I could be out making money?

The personalities of many of the metalheads make school even more disagreeable for them than it is for other students. As described in Chapter 4, many of them are high-sensation seekers and have personalities that thrive on aggressive activity. For such boys, the inaction of life in the classroom is a daily trial. This goes a long way toward explaining their deep antipathy for school and their bleak description of the school environment as one of forced passivity. "I just don't like being closed up for six hours," said Justin. "I don't like being inside, just sitting down," said Dan. "I'd rather be outside doing something. The classes I like best are art and gym, because I get up and do something."

For many, the only redeeming feature of school is that it is a place where they see their friends. Matt said he "hates schoolwork with a passion" but that he "likes it in the aspect that I get to see my friends." Similarly, Reggie said, "I don't like school, just the structure of it. But my high school's fun. All my friends are there." Algebra is the one class Rich likes, because "all my friends are in that class."

Not all boys had such scorn for school. Steve, who had just graduated from college and was considering graduate study in social work or psychology, said, "I'd be a student for the rest of my life if I could." But school was clearly a source of disgruntlement and alienation for many.

Thirty-one percent of the boys had a negative opinion of school, with 55 percent mixed or neutral and only 14 percent positive.[5] For the boys who hate it, their restless, active, high sensation-seeking personalities are constantly struggling against the structure and passivity of the classroom environment.

Keith Roe has done some interesting research on Swedish adolescents indicating that school failure (poor grades) is strongly related to liking heavy metal music.[6] He interprets this as indicating that failure in school causes children and adolescents to reject adult authority, which in turn leads them to associate with others who have failed and responded to this failure with resentment toward adults. These oppositional peer groups embrace oppositional music such as heavy metal as an expression of their alienation. School was certainly a source of alienation for the metalheads I interviewed, too, as the earlier examples indicate. However, unlike Roe, I do not think it is school failure per se that can be blamed for their dislike of school. On the contrary, I would reverse the direction of effects: It is not that they dislike school because they fail at it; rather, they fail at school because they dislike it, and they dislike it because the school environment does not actively involve them in learning that they perceive as useful and relevant to their present and future lives. American classrooms fail to inspire many students, but they are especially ill-designed for the active, aggressive, high sensation-seeking personality possessed by many metalheads.

Of course, it would be an oversimplification to say that the attitude that these boys have toward school and their experiences in school are due entirely to the school environment. As described in Chapter 6, the family environment many of the metalheads grew up in was characterized by a minimum of restraint, because of parents' beliefs that they should encourage the free expression of their child's inclinations to the greatest extent possible. One possible interpretation of the metalheads' frustration with the restrictive classroom environment is that they did not learn impulse control and self-restraint (that is, self-regulation) well enough in their family experience. Thus, they find themselves without these qualities in their repertoire when put into an environment—the classroom—where such qualities are necessary for success. "My personality is that I just can't take too many people giving me too many commands," explained Brad, a high school dropout. This is not to blame parents for the boys' difficulties with impulse control in school. The practices of families and schools in the majority culture of the United States are part of the larger pattern of broad socialization. Both families and schools take their cues from the larger culture, from the zeitgeist that prizes self-expression over self-restraint, self-esteem over self-control.

Neither parents, nor schools, nor the belief system of the American majority culture are likely to support a change toward tighter restraints and sterner discipline in the classroom. A more promising path may be to make the school environment more conducive to active learning. Adolescents' happiest moments in school come during active, participatory classes.[7] As noted above, American schools are unusual in the solitary and passive nature of their classroom environments. The emphasis on individual learning in American schools is well intended but misguided, and it does not work. Techniques that promote active, group-oriented, teacher-led learning have been proven effective in other countries and could be adapted for American schools. As it is now in the United States, the only choice for many adolescents is either to attend a boring, stifling high school or drop out. This Hobson's choice seems designed to kill the desire for education among adolescents.

Religion

One of the few near-universals among human cultures is that in virtually every place and in every era people engage periodically in religious activities. These activities take a fantastic variety of forms, but they are all clearly the same type of activity and have common characteristics. They always involve the supplication of supernatural beings or forces believed to hold great power over human affairs and natural phenomena. Solemn and strenuous efforts are made to gain the goodwill of these beings/forces, so that they will protect the worshippers from disease, hunger, natural disasters, and death, and so that they will provide the good things: food, health, children, victory over enemies. Also, religious activities typically involve *collective* rituals, rituals in which the entire clan or community is involved.[8] There is singing and dancing, musical instruments are played, great feasts are laid out. Penance is offered for inadequate worship of the supernatural beings; gratitude is poured forth for the favorable events. It is amazing how so many different cultures, in every corner of the world, with such different languages and economies and ways of life in such different environments, all seem to perform rituals of this kind in some form or other, almost without exception.

In this context, what is striking about the socialization environment of many American children is that religious beliefs and religious practices are *missing*. Even a comparison to the recent past in the United States is revealing.[9] The proportion of Americans who say religion is "very important" in their lives dropped from 75 percent in 1952 to 54 percent in 1987; for teens (aged 13–17) in 1987 the proportion was only 39 percent. In 1957, 69 percent of Americans saw the influence of religion in American life as increasing, whereas 14 percent saw it as decreasing; by 1988, 36 percent saw the influence of religion as increasing, whereas 48 percent saw it as decreasing. Teens, by a 2-to-1 margin, said that religion is less important to them than it is to their parents, in a 1987 survey. In this survey they also ranked religious faith *last* among eight values when they were asked whether it was "very important" for them to learn each of these values (Table 7.2).

Metalheads are, in a sense, the vanguard of this decline. Within a relatively unreligious generation they are even less religious than their peers. A high percentage of them—52 percent—describe themselves as atheists or agnostics,[10] compared to 11 percent in the comparison group.

There are several reasons for the unreligiousness of the metalheads. For one, they have embraced the American tradition of pluralism, of tolerance for the beliefs of others, so strongly that they have concluded not just that it is important to allow others to practice their beliefs without interference, but also that there are no important differences between one set of beliefs and another. With all of the immense variety of religious beliefs and practices that exist in the world, how could anyone manage to sort through them all and choose one as the truth or even as closer to the truth than others? Their socialization has not led them to prize one set of religious beliefs over all others but rather has left it up to them to find their own way among many choices. Under these circumstances, many of them have turned away altogether, overwhelmed by the abundance of options.

Listen to Reggie, for example:

> I don't see why I should commit myself to any one religion. There are so many religions out there and there's no way to tell. I mean, I read somewhere that

TABLE 7.2   Percentage of American Teenagers (aged 13–17) Calling Values "Very Important"

Value	Percentage
1. Honesty	89
2. Responsibility	89
3. Self-respect	87
4. Hard work	70
5. Independence	65
6. Patience	61
7. Obedience	60
8. Religious faith	44

NOTE: Table is reprinted by permission from Gallup and Castelli (1989), p. 130.

there's over a million religions in all, with all the different variations. And how can you know that one is just right? I'm not saying it's wrong to believe in religion, that's not what I'm saying at all. Each person should make their own decision when it comes to something like that.

Their education into pluralism makes them wary of accepting anything "on faith," that is, uncritically. They are skeptical of any claims that place religion above reasoned criticism. Henry put it this way:

I think it's unrealistic to take the Bible literally, because you gotta look at the time and the place and when it was written. It's very difficult to interpret. I think the Pope may be a good person to look to for at least a semiauthoritative view. Then again, who's to say that he's right? *[You don't think he's infallible?]* Oh, no. I mean, everyone makes mistakes.

A second reason many metalheads reject religion is that religious belief systems encourage conformity to one particular set of beliefs and values, and this is anathema to metalheads. Most belief systems state, implicitly, "These are the beliefs we should share and encourage others to share." In contrast, the belief system of individualism, shared by most Americans and taken to an extreme by the metalheads, states (implicitly) that "no one should be coerced or even encouraged to share the beliefs of others." Religions also traditionally advocate self-sacrifice and self-denial over self-fulfillment and self-expression, and this too is rejected by the metalheads—as it is increasingly by the rest of the majority culture, including religious authorities.[11] Metalheads resist the structure and limitation and control of religious organizations just as they resist the same type of efforts on the part of parents and schools. They feel that no one should try to mold them or influence them, as they refrain from trying to influence anyone else. They have no trustworthy reference point outside of themselves and their own feelings and desires, no way of evaluating the merits of competing views. Mark's statement exemplifies this:

I don't fall into any specific religious category. I believe in Christ, Muhammad, Buddha, Abraham, everybody. I believe they were all prophets of God. . . . I don't look down on anybody because their views on religion differ from mine, 'cause that's their own decision, their own choice. I believe in God, and that's about as far as it goes. [But] I don't like going to church because I don't like organized religion at all. I look at it as a medium for people to control everybody else's life.

Ron echoes this view, adding a knock on the acquisitiveness of religious institutions:

I believe in God, but I don't really believe in the churches or organized religion. I believe it's more of a personal thing. [*What don't you like about organized religion?*] Just the way it's organized, I guess. I don't think you should bring all these people together and have just one guy telling you what's a sin and what's not. . . . And the church, they acquire land and all this stuff, and they don't have to pay taxes. It seems like they're just another money-making corporation.[12]

The resistance among metalheads to religious socialization is actually quite similar to the views of the American public. George Gallup Jr. and Jim Castelli (1989), in a national survey of attitudes on religion, reported that the vast majority of Americans believe that individuals should arrive at their religious beliefs *independent of any church or synagogue*. The authors note that this is a view that has become more pervasive in recent decades. Increasingly, Americans see religious beliefs as something for each person to decide independently. They see religious institutions as a place to express their beliefs, but they resist the idea that such institutions should try to influence the content of those beliefs. Metalheads may be more resistant than others to religious socialization—if their lesser religiosity can be taken as evidence of this—but to a large extent they are only reflecting the resistance that exists in the American majority culture.

Their unreligiousness is also partly based on the mobility and instability of their family lives (discussed in Chapter 6). When a family moves from place to place every few years, it may come to seem pointless to form new ties in each new location, ties that will only have to be severed painfully before long. It is wearying to start over again and again in a new place. Eventually, families may decide that it is not worth it to make emotional investments in a neighborhood, community, school, or religious organization where they live, because all such ties are transient. Without the stability and consistency of growing up in one place, children develop no enduring tie to a particular church or synagogue, nor to the beliefs associated with it. One of the things that makes a certain set of religious beliefs important and meaningful is that the beliefs constitute one of the bonds between those who share them. The place of worship, too, develops significance as a place where you go to see people who know you well and like you and whom you know and like, people who do things for you and for whom you do things, people with whom you share ritual celebrations like weddings or bar mitzvahs. Without the residential stability that allows these ties to develop, ties to a religious organization and the beliefs it represents are also likely to remain stunted, lacking in emotional significance and power. The family history Jess described illustrates this:

I lived in California until I was about six or seven, and I went to church every Sunday. Then we moved to New Jersey and we went to church there. Now that we live in Atlanta, it's pretty much just Mother's Day and Christmas and Easter and things like that. My mom wants us to go, and I go [on these occasions] to make her happy. And every time I go to visit my grandparents in California, I go to church with them. But I'm not religious.

Perhaps Jess's comments reflect changes in religious observance that occur not only because of geographical mobility but because of growing up. The older children become, the more they become capable of resisting parents' attempts to recruit them to attend religious services. It may also be that parents feel a certain responsibility to introduce their children to religious observance and religious beliefs when the children are young,[13] but once children reach adolescence parents may feel they have done their duty and that it is up to the adolescent whether to continue to attend services or not. Michael, for example, was required to go to synagogue every week as a child, until his bar mitzvah at age thirteen. After that his parents no longer required him to go, and he stopped going. Billy, too, stopped attending religious services as soon as the inspiration of parental coercion was removed. "I used to go to church every Sunday, but since I've been in college I've just been too lazy."

Instability within the family can also be disruptive to the family's ties to a religious organization. "When my dad was living with us it was only natural that we went to church," said TJ. "And then once he moved out we stopped going." It may be that some families, or at least some of the individuals within a family, may rely especially strongly on the support of their religious organization when they are going through a divorce. It is easy to see, however, that it would be difficult for all members of a family to continue to attend the same place of worship in the aftermath of a divorce. There may also be a sense of humiliation or shame that leads families to withdraw from participation in the religious organization following a divorce, particularly in denominations where divorce is condemned. And divorce often brings with it geographical changes that would also act to disrupt ties to the place of worship. Whatever the specific reasons, Gallup and Castelli (1989) find that divorced and/or single parents are less likely than other parents to provide their children with religious training.

With religion, as with other aspects of their lives, there is diversity among the metalheads, and there are some of them who do not fit the general pattern and are more conventionally religious. For the most part, however, religion does not hold any strong emotional significance for them one way or the other. The beliefs for which so many have lived and died over the course of centuries, which have inspired some people to great feats of love and courage, inspired some to acts of appalling cruelty and brutality, and made others shiver and cower with dread and fear, provoke only a tepid reaction from most metalheads. Scott, for example:

I really don't worry about heaven and hell, because I figure I'm OK if there is or isn't. I'm OK just rotting in the ground when I die. If I go to heaven, then I'm happy. If I go to hell, I'll deal with it when it comes.

To Scott, as for most metalheads, and in fact for the majority of adolescents growing up in the contemporary West, organized religion has little more relevance to their lives than the horse and carriage have as a mode of transportation.

If metalheads generally reject traditional and organized religion, they do not leap to satanism as a substitute, notwithstanding the popular perception and the occasional sensationalized account in the media. Ironically, their cynicism about conventional religion carries over to satanism as well, and to the attempts by some heavy metal bands to present themselves as satanic. When I asked them about the reputation of heavy metal for promoting satanism, the question was greeted with derision, almost without exception. "I laugh at it," said Peter. "It's funny because it's all a fake, a gimmick to get them ahead." "People ask me if I'm a satanist because I like metal," said James. "I just say, 'You've watched too many Geraldo specials.' Because no heavy metal band really believes in Satan. It's all a ploy to sell albums." This was the most common perspective: that the "satanism" of some heavy metal bands is not only something few metalheads believe in but something the performers themselves do not believe; they are only using it as a promotional device of sorts. As Ron observed, "Bands do it to make people go 'Oh my God, did you hear what he said?' and get people to listen to their music." Derek scoffed, "It's just a gag, a promotional kind of thing. I mean, I'm sure they don't go home and slay calves on weekends." The metalheads are not deceived, even if they do buy the albums. They allow this as an exception to the authenticity that they otherwise demand of their heavy metal heroes. It should be added that satanic themes are actually quite rare in heavy metal songs (as the song analysis contained in Chapter 3 showed).

Most metalheads may not have a religion, but they do have a belief system of sorts, an ideology: the ideology of alienated individualism. It is revealing that proclamations of individualism often came in response to questions about their religious beliefs. "I believe in individuals and I believe in me," said Miles when I asked him how he would describe himself religiously. Brian responded similarly: "I have no religious anything. I'm not antireligious, but I think that if people like it that's a personal choice. I choose to believe in myself more than any religion." Even Lew, the one self-described satanist in the study, was ultimately a proponent of individualism: "People have to meet halfway no matter what their religions are. I'm not against Christians. Everybody has their own thing."

Proclamations of individualism were also delivered by some of them when they were asked to describe themselves *politically*, indicating that

"The Satanic Army" logo, a satire on the Salvation Army logo, shows the ironic attitude most metalheads take toward the claim that heavy metal promotes satanism.

their individualism is an ideology that applies to many aspects of their lives. "My motto is you should be able to do whatever you want as long as you don't hurt anybody else," said Reggie. This is the metalhead motto, the heart of the metalhead ideology. "I'm a personal anarchist," said Dan, when I asked him to describe himself politically. "You should do what you feel is right and what you believe in. Anything goes until it goes so far as to hurt others."

Heavy metal provides the hymns and anthems for their belief system of alienated individualism.[14] To put it another way, alienated individualism is the belief system that underlies heavy metal music. The metalheads are united in their resistance to being unified, they collect in great concert halls to celebrate their rejection of anything collective. The concerts provide the ritual celebration of their ideology, and the lyrics of the songs provide the text that articulates and legitimizes their beliefs.

Friends

Bereft of ties to a community of people who know them and whom they also know, having only loose ties to their families, lacking in ties to a religious organization where they are known and valued, adolescents' ties to friends take on a magnified significance. True, because of the high mobility of American families, adolescents' ties to friends may be shattered suddenly and painfully, as the examples in the previous chapter showed. However, friends can also provide solace and refuge from family chaos and disintegration, and also an emotional foothold in a new place. For some boys, a mutual enthusiasm for heavy metal can provide the basis for a new friendship, a source of connection and common ground for two adolescents who are otherwise unknown to each other. It is a notable feature of contemporary American life that in the midst of all the high mobility, the repeated pulling up of roots and moving to another place that so many families undergo, media such as television and music provide a foundation of shared experience that extends from coast to coast and from border to border. For an adolescent metalhead, wherever his family moves, anywhere in the country, he can be assured that somewhere in his new community are other boys who are fellow metal devotees, who have listened to the same recordings, watched the same music videos, and attended concerts by the same bands as he has. Scott described how his relationship with his best friend began:

> We met through a friend of my parents. He lived right down the street, so that was convenient. We kind of blossomed together. We both discovered what we could do and who we could be at the same time, and we shared the same aspirations and goals. We both liked metal, too; that was the initial thing we could talk about. It gave us something to talk about to start out with.

For Steve, heavy metal has been a way of identifying others who share his sense of alienation.

> I never felt I fit in with most of the normal people. I would never fit in with the athletes or the smart people or the well-dressed ones. I always felt like an outcast, so I hung out with the outcasts. [Heavy metal] is something that attracts us together and helps us be friends.

In listening to Dan, one can hear the role of the heavy metal concert event in promoting and intensifying friendships.

> [Before concerts] we all want to get out as soon as we can just to be with each other. You can get really high just on being with friends. We'll get to the show early and just hang out outside and talk to each other.

It is not true, however, that a mutual enthusiasm for heavy metal is either absolutely necessary or entirely sufficient for a metalhead to form a friendship. According to Mitch, his best friends are "the smart kids," and they don't care for heavy metal at all. Only one-half of the metalheads said that most or all of their friends also like heavy metal; the other half said that some, few, or none of their friends like it. Even vehement disagreement about music does not necessarily impede a friendship. As Scott said of his friends and their attitudes toward heavy metal:

> They either like it or really hate it. Most of them like it, but there are definitely those who hate it and plug their ears and force me to listen to their music. It's a constant battle, so we just turn the radio off.

In some cases disagreement about music can even *promote* friendship, as friends spend hours debating whose music is superior. For Ben, whose family moved around so much during his growing up, comparing musical interests has been a way of beginning new friendships, whether the comparison results in disagreement or the identification of fellow metalheads:

> Actually, my best friend likes the Beatles. The Beatles and the Who. When we first met it was like every day we'd always argue about who's better. . . . I guess most of my friends like heavy metal, but that's not really a quality I look for in a person. It's a great way to meet people, though. You'll see a person wearing a heavy metal t-shirt or something, and people will come up to him, "Hey, did you go to the show?"

However, friendship is not always a source of solidarity and consolation. Like family relationships, friendships can dissolve and leave bitterness; like family members, friends can disappoint, deceive, and betray. For Jack, his experience of being betrayed by a friend has heightened his sense of alienation and contributed to his hyperindividualism. One day he came home to find that the person he had thought of as his best friend for four years, whom he had been allowing to stay rent-free in the house where he lived with his mother, had stolen $350 cash and another $300 worth of Jack's tapes.

Concerts are wusually attended with friends. (Photo by Nick Romanenko)

Stole it all and disappeared. I trusted him. You know somebody for four years, you think you can trust them. I thought he was like my brother. I don't care now about the tapes and the money, it's just that it really hurt me. I felt real close to him, I felt like I could tell him anything. . . . That's why I really don't trust nobody.

Friendship, too, can be a source of the alienated individualism metalheads feel and find expression for in heavy metal music.

*   *   *

Western societies have embarked unwittingly upon a vast and unprecedented natural experiment. The question under investigation is, What happens if you take human beings, who have in all societies at all times been enveloped in a social structure of one kind or another, and remove that structure except for the barest skeleton? What kind of human beings result? Take away the elaborate structure of family ties that other societies have—grandparents, uncles, aunts, cousins, great-uncles, great-aunts, second cousins, numerous siblings, and so on—and leave only a denuded "nuclear family" of father, mother, and perhaps one sibling; or perhaps even leave out father and siblings, perhaps only mother and child. Take away ties to the community, neighbors whose ties to the family extend back generations and who have known the current generation of children since birth, neighbors who perhaps take a particular interest in a particular child because of similarities in talents, interests, or personality; leave only the mildest nodding acquaintance between neighbors who barely know each others' names and who gather all of their belongings every few years and move somewhere else far away. Now take away the overarching structure of beliefs that explain how life began, what the significance of a human life is, and what lies beyond the veil of life into death.

What remains is, in one sense, an unprecedented freedom for individuals. Let us be careful not to romanticize traditional societies with their elaborate structure of relationships and prohibitions and obligations. If this is comforting and guiding, it is also limiting and at times oppressive. We are free of those strictures now, freer than ever before to work out our own destinies. Individuals are allowed and even encouraged to develop their unique talents and interests, to follow their own inclinations wherever they might lead—"to do whatever you want as long as you don't hurt anybody else," as Reggie put it. This results in a spectacular variety of forms of human experience, as a broad range of variability in talents and interests among individuals is allowed expression. Society is more creative, vibrant, and energetic as a consequence.

At the same time, however, it is important to note the costs of such freedom, and also what has been lost in the course of shedding traditional ways. If it is true that in our time individuals have greater freedom to choose their own direction in life, it is also true that more people end up aimless. Without having a path provided for them, lacking the personal resources to find one of their own, they end up disoriented, lost. If it is true that parents treat children more gently and with greater consideration for their psychological well-being in our time as compared with the past, it is also true that children are much more likely to experience instability in their family lives—divorce and remarriage, repeated geographical relocations. Before this century children more often lost a parent due to death while the children were still young, but a divorce is often worse than a death because children often experience it amid the furious acrimony of the parents. They find themselves ripped apart emotionally as they are caught in the crossfire of their parents' hatred, an excruciating and tremendously destructive experience.

And if it is true that children are encouraged to develop their abilities and express themselves, in contrast to the sometimes cruel and humorless inculcation of guilt and self-denial characteristic of the past, it is also true that sometimes this encouragement takes place at the expense of teaching self-regulation and consideration for others. When children are encouraged to express themselves without reservation, to feel good about themselves without relation to their actions, the results may be disastrous. Not everything that flows out of the human heart merits expression, and people who feel good about themselves even though they behave selfishly eventually cause serious trouble for others and often for themselves.

Heavy metal is about this dark side of modernity. It speaks to those who have been provided unprecedented freedom, in particular those who feel the exhilaration of that freedom but also the insecurity of it, the sense that they are on their own, for better or worse. It speaks to those who are proudly individualistic but who also feel the loneliness of that individualism. It speaks to many of the adolescents of a generation that is growing up without the traditional supports of extended family, community, and religion. Not only does it speak *to* them; it also speaks, or rather shouts and screams, on their behalf. It is the angry shout of those who have reacted to the absence of these traditional supports and sources of meaning with a deep cynicism about the trustworthiness and reliability of the world around them.

Jean

Jean was dressed entirely in black the day of the interview, from her black leather boots to her black jeans and black t-shirt (with a heavy metal logo on it). She was slim and well groomed, and her complexion was pale, contrasting sharply with her black clothes and her dark hair. This was not unusual dress for her; in fact, she said she wore all black all the time. "It's always been my favorite color," she explained. "Most of my wardrobe has been black for four years."

Many metalheads frequently wear black t-shirts with logos from heavy metal bands, but to wear black from head to toe, every day, carries the motif one step further. Black is the color of mourning, and Jean seemed depressed, as if in mourning for her younger hopes of what the world would be like or what her life would be like. She seemed to have withdrawn from the world to a large extent, and now kept only the most tenuous and superficial ties to others. "I'm not a very social person," she said. "I have a hard time expressing myself."

Her social isolation came up with regard to several different topics, including school, friends, and family. A sophomore in college, she usually kept to herself at school. "It's not a social place for me, really, as much as it is for a lot of people. You can tell when you meet somebody if they're going to be a compatible person to talk to. I don't find very many people like that, at least not in my classes." Even in her relationships with friends she tended to keep them at arm's length emotionally. When unhappy or upset she tended to push them away rather than confide in them. "I withdraw completely," she said. "That's the last time I want to talk about anything. Even if they come out and ask me, I'll only say what I'm comfortable with, or I'll just shut them off completely and just say 'I'm sorry, I really don't want to talk about it.'" She found it safer to keep her feelings inside and not let anyone know too much. "I suppose if you put all my friends together and they put their two bits about me together, they'd have a decent part of the picture, but all together I don't think anyone has the whole picture. I like to be like that. If you tell too much, you get in trouble."

Her family life was not unhappy, but her family relationships had this same quality of distance, the same undercurrent of distrust. She described her relationship with her mother as "very casual. We get along very well, but I wouldn't say we sit and talk about it too much." Her mother was an alcoholic, and this condition was sometimes a source of conflict between them—conflict Jean typically reacted to by withdrawing. "She does very well with it sometimes," she said of her mother, "but there are other times that she goes off the handle and I can't handle it, so I just either leave or we have a few words and I just go." Her father had died of cancer about a year ago, and that had been a big blow to her. "My dad was my favorite person," she said. They had not talked much, either, but she had felt an unspoken closeness to him. "Me and my dad could hang out for hours on end, and almost not even speak to each other but really get along. I mean, it could be about the weather or the family, but we were very connected. Very close."

She was the youngest of nine children, and she said she got along well with her brothers and sisters. "I'm never mad at any of them, and we never really fight." Still, she kept them from getting close to her in the same way she kept her friends away; in fact, she compared her relationships with her siblings to friendships. "It's more like along the idea of a friendship, not confidence or trusting them with anything more than a dime. I don't confide in them very much. My sisters, I do to a point, but there's always a stopping point. There's tons of things I just won't say."

For her as for so many metalheads, heavy metal music was a beacon in the dark night of her alienation. She could hear the echo of her own voice in the angry rantings of heavy metal singers in songs portraying loneliness, frustration, deception, and betrayal. "They can express it and I can't," she said. "I've never been able to express my feelings." Through heavy metal songs she found vicarious expression for all the tortured feelings she felt she could not share with anyone else. Although she kept her feelings bottled up tight, she envied heavy metal performers who could shout them out loud. "I've got a lot of feelings that I wish I could express.

Sometimes I wish I could be open like that. Sometimes I feel trapped and I wish I could just let it out like that."

She was frustrated by her tendency to inhibit and enclose her feelings, but it made her feel better to listen to heavy metal performers who could "let it out." The cathartic effect of the music, so common among the boys, was something she experienced as well. "I think it takes out my aggressions," she said. "If I'm in an aggressive mood, I think it sort of calms me down." She understood the songs to be on "depressing" themes, but she saw the songs as purging both the depression and the aggression that might result from being depressed. "There is sometimes a depressing tone [to the songs] as well as aggression; because they're depressed, they're aggressive. I don't act that way, but it actually makes me feel better that someone does. . . . I think it puts me in a better mood, to tell you the truth."

Jean was lonely, with little in her life to relieve her loneliness but heavy metal. In contrast to many of the boys, her alienation was turned inward rather than outward. She was not reckless in her automobile driving, sexual behavior, drug use, or anything else. Her alienation from family and peers at school was characterized more by detachment than anger. She was simply unhappy, and she seemed to be suffering from a kind of emotional malnourishment that she did not know how to relieve.

Other than heavy metal music, the one joy in her life seemed to be her love of children. She was majoring in early childhood education in college, and she planned a career in child care. Asked to name three people she admired, she said, "Any child, because they are so innocent. I just admire the innocence and purity of children, I guess." She was adamantly against abortion because "it's not the child's fault. The baby did nothing wrong, and they shouldn't have to suffer." Although love was missing in her own life, she nevertheless hoped to be able to provide it to children. "I enjoy taking care of children. I just think they need as much attention as they can get."

Summary profile: Jean

Age: 19
Race: White

Education: sophomore in college

Current occupation: works in florist's shop

Father's occupation: deceased

Mother's occupation: nurse

Family background: youngest of nine children, father died of cancer one year ago, mother an alcoholic

Spent most of childhood in: Boston

Number of heavy metal recordings owned: 50

Favorite heavy metal groups: Metallica, Skid Row, Queensrÿche

Goals in ten years: married, career in child care

Political orientation: "I don't get into politics very much"

Religious orientation: Catholic, but does not attend church

Hobbies/leisure preferences: pewter collection of sorcerers and dragons; taking care of children

Number of times in past year:

Driven a car under the influence of alcohol:	0
Driven a car over 80 miles per hour:	1
Driven a car greater than 20 mph over speed limit:	1
Had sex without contraception:	0
Had sex with someone not known well:	0
Used marijuana:	1
Used cocaine:	0
Damaged or destroyed public or private property:	0
Shoplifted:	0

The Girls of Metal

The "absence" of girls from masculinist subcultures is not very surprising. These subcultures in some form or other explore and celebrate masculinity, and as such eventually relegate girls to a subordinate place within them. They reflect the sexism of the outside world.

—**Michael Brake,** *Comparative Youth Culture*

Heavy metal is largely a male domain. The performers as well as the fans are predominantly male, and, as described in Chapter 1, there are elements of the subculture that are distinctively related to maleness and manhood. In particular, the concert scene exalts traditionally male virtues of toughness and aggressiveness (through the music as well as through slamdancing). More generally, the high-sensation intensity of the music appeals more to males, with their generally higher appetites for sensation.

However, there are also adolescent girls whose sensation-seeking tendencies are high enough for heavy metal music to appeal to them. Furthermore, the alienation that draws so many of the boys to heavy metal also exists among some girls, and they, too, find an ideological home in the subculture of heavy metal. In this chapter on the girls of heavy metal,[1] we shall see that in many respects they share similarities with the male metalheads. Like the boys, the allure of heavy metal for girls includes not only the high-sensation qualities of the music, but also their admiration for the prowess of heavy metal musicians and the dream of involving themselves in the world of heavy metal performance in one way or another. Also, the alienation from family, school, and religion that is common among the boys is also common among girls who like heavy metal, and they are drawn to heavy metal because it both expresses and alleviates their alienation.

However, they differ from the boys in some important ways. Sexual issues are involved in the appeal of heavy metal for girls, as they often become involved in it through a boyfriend or because of the sexual attraction they feel for the performers or fans. Also, as girls they have an additional source of alienation in the exploitation and denigration of women that sometimes takes place in American society—and in some heavy metal songs. Many of them are aware that girls are a small and not always respected minority in the world of heavy metal, and they struggle to reconcile their enthusiasm for heavy metal with their sense of being not quite welcome in that world.

The allure of heavy metal: The girls' view

For the most part, the girls sound remarkably similar to the boys when they talk about the appeal of heavy metal. Just as for the boys, the primary themes are the high-sensation pleasures of the music, admiration for the skill of the performers, and their sense of identification with the alienation expressed in the songs.

The novelty and intensity of the songs appeal to high sensation-seeking girls, just as to high sensation-seeking boys. Holly said she became interested in Metallica's music because "the way it sounded was different than anything else." She contrasted this with "the traditional love songs," which are "all the same, over and over again." Karen said she likes heavy metal for "the heaviness of it. I like the loudness of it, basically." Christine likes the way the bass guitar, "if it's really loud, kind of affects your heartbeat and stuff." Girls who like heavy metal rate themselves as higher in sensation seeking on the kinds of items described in Table 4.1, compared to other girls.[2]

Many of the girls also admire the musical expertise of the performers. "It's very intricate music," said Nina. "It's very difficult. You really have to practice to be good at it. The musicians are extremely talented." A surprisingly high proportion of the girls (37 percent) aspire to a career involving music, either as a performer or in some other respect. This proportion is much higher than the girls in the comparison group (5 percent), and it is equal to the proportion of the male metalheads (36 percent) aspiring to music-oriented careers (see Chapter 5). What makes it surprisingly high among the girls is that currently so few females are employed in the heavy metal "business." Virtually all of the performers are male, and the production, distribution, and administrative aspects of the business are also dominated by men.[3] Girls like Shanelle hope to break in anyway.

> I would really like to work for a record company doing something serious: promotion, maybe managing. It's a big dream, because girls don't get into that very easily, and you have to be taken seriously, and there aren't too many positions open. I'd prefer to be in a band, but that's kind of a dream thing.

Several of the girls mentioned other artistic aspirations. Connie hoped to open an art store. Christine saw herself "living in a farm in a kind of

A female fan and friend. (Photo by Nick Romanenko)

artists' community" in ten years. Amy believed her destiny was as a "starving artist, possibly an illustrator." Holly said that in ten years she would "probably be dead on the street if I'm not doing something with art. I like drawing, sculpture, painting, photography, performing, and theater arts." Thus part of the allure of heavy metal for girls may be that it represents an alternative way of life, one that is more creative and unconventional than the lifestyle offered in the mainstream American middle class. This is also evident in the aspirations of the boys (for example, Reggie, whose profile precedes Chapter 7).

However, what distinguishes the girls from the boys in their attraction to heavy metal is that for the girls, sexual and romantic elements are involved. Several of them said they had become interested in heavy metal through a boyfriend who was a metalhead. "He was a musician, and he was in a band," Nina said of her former boyfriend. "[Heavy metal] was the most important thing to him, and that's how it became a very important part of my life." Many of them mentioned the attractiveness of the performers and/or the fans in explaining why they liked heavy metal. Jennifer had become interested through seeing heavy metal videos on MTV. "I noticed, God, these guys are kind of attractive, in a weird sort of way, and that's how I started listening to it." She had met her current boyfriend at a concert.

Going to a concert puts them in a situation where they are surrounded by available young men. Often, they go with a group of males. Connie said the group who went to a recent concert consisted of "myself and five guys. I was the only girl." The reason for this is that not many girls like metal. "More often I go with a guy," said Jean, "because most of my girlfriends don't get into it." If they do go with a girlfriend, it may be with the hope of meeting boys. Lynn preferred to go to concerts without her boyfriend, so she could enjoy flirting with other young men there. "If I have a boyfriend, I won't go to a concert with him. There are some good-looking guys there!" she said. Sarah had a similar view: "Sometimes I go with just a girlfriend of mine, especially if we feel like scoping on the hot men." Some of them spoke of dressing to attract. "We try new looks for concerts," said Kelly. "We'll call each other and say, 'I have this new look for my hair, we can try this or that.'"

It is important to note, however, that the girls are deeply divided on the idea of the heavy metal concert as a place for meeting males. Many of the girls like going to concerts for the same reasons as the boys: to enjoy the high-sensation spectacle of it and admire the prowess of the musicians. There are some who dress to attract boys and go with the hope and intention of meeting them, and others who despise the girls whom they see as too blatant in their sexual display. Karen said she usually goes to concerts with men because "the metal women that dress up, I wouldn't want to hang around them anyway." Shanelle put it most strongly:

The bimbos [at concerts] are disgusting. Girls who go dressed like that to heavy metal concerts, wear their little short skirts up to here when they know there's gonna be some guy behind her putting his hand up her skirt, you're asking for trouble. I mean, you can dress up nice, but get a clue. I would never dress like that. [Why do they do it?] Attention. Serious attention. Honestly, I think a lot of girls that I've known who dress like that, and in my opinion are a

Most of the girls don't mind that the ratio of boys to girls at concerts is heavily in favor of the boys. (Photo by Nick Romanenko)

bunch of sleazebags, they were not raised properly, or their parents wouldn't let them walk out of the house like that. Some of the guys are really cute, so I can see why they would want to attract them, and it works. They're the ones going home with someone, and I'm not.

Alienation in the lives of the girls

The alienation that is so vivid in the lives of the boys is also present in the lives of the girls. It has some of the same sources for the girls as it does for the boys: tenuous or conflicted attachments to family, school, and religion. The girls, like the boys, see heavy metal as an expression of their alienation, and also as a way of relieving it. However, the girls have an important source of alienation that the boys do not: their sense that they may face exploitation and denigration simply for being female.

The girls spoke of estrangement from their parents in stories similar to those of the boys. "Me and my dad cannot be talking without fighting," said Lynn. "We just do not agree on anything. I mean, if it's dinner we'll argue about how something is supposed to be made. We'll argue about what time a TV show's supposed to be on. I mean, we just can't be together without fighting." Overall, female metalheads reported more troubled family relationships on a questionnaire concerning family relationships, compared to other girls.[4] For them as for the boys, divorce was sometimes an important source of alienation. "When my dad moved out it was pretty hard; all my grades went down," said Anne. In the aftermath she harbors a great deal of anger and resentment toward him. "He's an idiot," she said of her father, who has a Ph.D. in chemistry. "He's childish and immature. We don't get along. I don't like my dad and he doesn't like me, and we're happy that way."

At least as much as for the boys, heavy metal is a source of conflict between the girls and their parents. Part of this, as for the boys, results from the fact that the high-sensation qualities of heavy metal that appeal so much to some adolescents are the very qualities that their parents find disagreeable.[5] "My parents never liked any sort of loud music," said Kristin. "They yell at me to lower it and stuff, because they can't really see it as music; they just see it as noise." Hannah said that her mother objects to heavy metal because "anything that's not Perry Como is too much for her." Like the parents of boys, the parents of girls are rarely successful in their efforts to discourage their children's involvement in the music or the subculture. Shanelle said that her mother "was not happy" about her enthusiasm for heavy metal, "but she learned to live with it after a while, because I told her, 'This is me, take it or leave it.'" Connie said that her parents "just kind of look at it and sigh and walk away. Occasionally my dad will walk in and I'll be watching 'Headbanger's Ball' [on MTV]. He'll just stand and look at it for a while and then he'll give me this weird look and walk away."

The girls, like the boys and many other American students, consider school to be a dreary duty. Kristin described school as "pretty confining. I think it's good to learn, but it's not very realistic and sometimes it's not very encouraging either." Amy said that she does well in school, "but it's more of an obligation. Usually I find it very easy, but some of the stuff gets really pointless. My favorite times of the day are before school and after school, because that's when I hang around with my friends." Being with friends is the one consolation school provides. "I like it because my friends are there," said Sharon. "And I hate it because I'm not interested in schoolwork." "I like classes for who's in the classes, not for what we do in the classes," said Tracy. "I like classes my friends are in."

The girls also echoed the boys in their rejection of organized religion. They were more likely than girls in the comparison group to describe themselves as agnostics or atheists,[6] and even when they described themselves as religious or "spiritual" it was usually in an unorthodox way. Their pluralism and relativism make them regard all organized religion as equally remote and irrelevant to their lives. Shanelle said, "I don't have a religion, because I don't know exactly what each religion believes in." "I don't say it's wrong," said Karen, "but there's so many people that believe in so many different gods, how can there be just one?" Christine declared herself an agnostic. "I was raised in a Jewish family, but I don't consider myself Jewish now because I don't believe in Judaism or any other organized religion. I think there's truth in almost all religions, but I also think there's a lot of misguided lessons in all of them."

They also see organized religion as threatening intolerable restraints on their individualism.[7] Tina said she believes in God, "but I don't believe in organized religion. I think you can worship God and be religious without someone saying you have to do this and this and this." Sarah said that she believes in God, "but I don't like having rules and regulations of 'you can't do this' and 'you can't do that.'" In addition, they see organized religion as corrupt and hypocritical. Tracy said she considers herself "a spiritual person. I believe there's a God and everything, but personally I'd just rather not go to church. I think it's kind of hypocritical." For Nina, although she was raised in the Catholic religion, she no longer considers herself part of it because "I think with the Catholic church, there is corruption in everything. It really saddens me to see that the Catholic church is hypocritical. There's a lot of corruption and dirt there."

Alienation and heavy metal: The girls' view

Although the girls' interest in heavy metal often begins with a boyfriend who likes the music or with their sexual attraction to heavy metal performers or fans, many of them also respond to the message of alienated individualism that is expressed in heavy metal songs. Amy, for example, admired the defiantly individualistic quality of Metallica's early work: "It's sort of like 'We're going to do it our way. You can't tell us what to do because we know what's right for us.'" Several of the girls contrasted heavy metal songs with other, more superficial kinds of songs. "Heavy metal songs make so much more sense than a dance song," said Jean. Kristin said that heavy metal "has a lot of feeling to it, you know. I don't find it to be full of shit." The songs take on serious, important topics. "[Heavy metal] songs tend to be more about real stuff," said Heidi.

The same paradoxical effect described by the boys was described by the girls. Heavy metal songs reaffirm their sense that the world is a hopeless mess, but at the same time the songs comfort them by confirming that they are not alone in their disillusionment. "It usually makes me feel better when I'm feeling cynical about the state of the world," said Christine. "It somehow kind of reassures my own beliefs and makes me feel like I'm not the only one who feels that way and that other people care enough to write songs about it." They find comfort and consolation in hearing someone else express the alienation and loneliness that they feel but sometimes have difficulty expressing. "It makes me feel better because I'm not the only one that thinks like this and there's other people out there," said Karen. "If they can write a song that can say exactly what I was trying to think, then obviously I'm not the only one that thinks something like that."

Heavy metal not only provides this consolation to them, it also purges their anger and sadness. Sixty-three percent of them said they listen to heavy metal especially when they are angry or sad, and nearly all of these girls—close to half of all female metalheads—said the music had a cathartic effect, soothing them and calming them down. The language they used to describe it was similar to that of the boys. "When I'm pissed off I listen to it a lot," said Sharon. "It's the only way I can release my tension without hitting something. . . . It puts me in a better mood if I'm mad. Because I can listen to it, and calm down, and I'll be OK." Shanelle said she listens to metal because of "the aggression. Everybody needs to get it out. That's how I think kids do it. That's how I do it." Joanne described how heavy metal intensifies her anger, then sweeps it away. "If I'm in a bad mood, sometimes I listen to it. It gets me more angry, but by the time I'm done listening to it, it gets my anger out." Anne listed the moods that lead her to listen to metal and used a creative analogy to describe the effect. "Anger, fright, sadness, extreme sadness, boredom. If I'm really mad, it will alleviate some of that anger. It's like what a masseuse does on your back to loosen up the muscles. It's just pounding it in. It relaxes me. It alleviates some of the tension." Rather than being a cause of aggressive or reckless behavior, heavy metal is more likely to be an alternative to it for the girls, as it is for the boys.[8] "It's good for blowing off steam. Instead of yelling and throwing things, you can turn something up really loud," said Heidi. "Sometimes if I'm hyper or something it'll help me calm down. I mean, they can scream and curse and say all these things that I would never say or never do, but they can do it and I can listen."

In addition to the sources of alienation they share with the boys, the girls have a source of alienation that the boys do not: The treatment of women in what they see as a male-dominated world. Ironically, the girls see certain heavy metal songs as prime examples of and contributors to contempt and disrespect toward women. As noted in the song analysis contained in Chapter 3, male-female themes are relatively rare in heavy metal songs, but when females do appear in the songs they are frequently described with anger, fear, and exploitation. However, the bands the girls seem to have in mind when they are critical of heavy metal's depiction of women are bands that the boys often see as "poseurs," the "glam rock" or "glam metal" bands, or as practitioners of hard rock—in any case, bands that are not true heavy metal bands. Amy made the distinction explicit. "I really dislike songs [that portray women negatively], but I find mostly that it's less in heavy metal that that happens, than it is in like rap or glam rock. It makes me mad when that's classified as heavy metal because there's an attitude with heavy metal . . . the honesty and stuff . . . and these bands just do not have it; they're out there to make a buck, or they're out there to get girls." Karen was among several girls who made it clear that glam metal is not the type of metal they listen to. "Most of the stuff that I listen to, there aren't any videos with women, there aren't any songs against women or whatever. The bands like that, I think I kind of more laugh it off because I try to think of where the source came from and think 'Well, look at you. You look like a woman and you're calling me names and saying bad things about me. Obviously you have problems to be saying stuff like that.'"

Karen could dismiss it like this, even laugh it, but many of the other girls reacted with outrage and resentment. The vehemence of many of the girls on this topic was striking. Tina said she found Guns N' Roses "downright filthy. They're vulgar, and gross, and dirty, and they sing nasty songs. I just personally hate them. They're vile and repulsive. . . . I don't think it's good for young boys to grow up in this, and even worse, young females listen to this. How are they going to grow up and let themselves be treated? The female is portrayed as some sex toy, that's all there is." Nina also worried about the effects of such songs on young people. "Women are not taken seriously among a lot of heavy metal bands. Like the big-hair bands [that is, glam metal or hard rock bands], they just portray women very cheaply, really disrespectfully. . . . It gets me really afraid when I see people cheering at some of the lyrics, especially people my age and younger. I think for younger people, it could have an effect on how they treat women in the future." Kristin was more angry than afraid: "Any metal video I've ever seen, it's just tits and ass; that's like all that it is. The metal boys from high school who are sitting back watching these videos, they're probably going to get some twisted image of women, completely idealized and ridiculous. . . . Somebody should shoot Axl Rose in the knee."

Other girls struggled with their recognition that some heavy metal songs have exploitative portrayals of women, and they simultaneously criticized such songs and excused them. Jennifer exemplified this struggle:

A lot of bands [denigrate women], but it's just been a part of the way people think for so long, that probably they're not thinking about it. But they're not helping it any, by not thinking about it. Maybe they do contribute to it. I guess sometimes I take offense, and other times I don't. . . . If they put women in their videos who look a certain way, that's fine, because these women did not have to agree to it, either. A lot of people will say, "Look how they demoralize women by putting them in their videos." But they didn't have to agree to be in the videos, so they are both to blame.

Other girls tried to explain the exploitation of women in some heavy metal songs by observing that the exploitation of women is simply a pervasive fact of life. Sally said metal songs were no worse than most other songs. "I think every song is [antiwomen]. I mean, every fucking rap song is." To Nina, the portrayal of women in metal songs was simply a reflection of reality. "I think the world is antiwomen. There is so much in everyday life that I come across. I think it is a male-dominated world and I think it will always be that way."

For girls, then, heavy metal is a source of alienation as well as a source of relief from it. Although some heavy metal relieves their alienation and provides a consoling expression for it, some of the songs and bands on the fringes of heavy metal, especially the glam metal bands that are closer to hard rock, also deepen their alienation and confirm their sense that the adult world they are about to enter is a grim and perilous place.

Girls and boys

Girls tend to be on the periphery of youth subcultures,[9] and this is particularly true of the heavy metal subculture. Classroom surveys,[10] including the one used in this study, indicate that fewer girls than boys like heavy metal. As noted here and in Chapter 1, heavy metal concerts are attended almost entirely by boys, although this can be part of the attraction for the girls who do attend. In part, the greater appeal of heavy metal for boys reflects higher average levels of sensation seeking among boys.[11] Heavy metal appeals only to people who have a high tendency for sensation seeking. Because boys, in general, are higher than girls in sensation seeking, more boys are in this category and more boys like heavy metal.

Does the greater appeal of heavy metal for boys also reflect greater alienation among boys as compared to girls? There is no simple answer to this question. Generalizations about gender usually oversimplify, and they obscure more than they illuminate. Comparing one half of the human population to the other half inevitably glosses over the enormous variability that exists within each half.

The question is difficult to answer, and perhaps there is no point in answering it. Perhaps it is enough to state that alienation is pervasive among American adolescents, male and female alike. Boys are more likely to be attracted to heavy metal, because they are higher in sensation seeking, and heavy metal music provides high-sensation expression and relief for their alienation. But many girls, too, suffer from a sense of isolation and loneliness. Many girls, too, are alienated from socializing institutions of family, community, school, and religion. Because of the radically individualistic nature of their socialization, many young people of each gender are moving into adulthood poorly prepared for the demands of impulse control, mutual obligation, and self-regulation that are inherent in adult roles. This topic will be explored further in the final chapter.

PROFILE

Barry

Barry had long, curly, nicely groomed black hair. His features were dark; during the interview he said he was mainly of Peruvian and Italian ancestry, with some Irish and Polish as well. He had a muscular build, which was accented by the sleeveless black shirt he was wearing. It looked like he had not shaved in a while; there was maybe a week's worth of growth to his beard, all of it jet black.

There was a fierce intensity about him. He spoke emphatically and passionately about everything that came up in the interview, as if he contained a tremendous energy that surfaced no matter what the topic. He was intelligent and thoughtful. However, he also seemed restless and erratic, as if he were barely in control of the energy he possessed.

His life was in disarray. He had been fired from his job that morning. During the past week he had either missed work or arrived late nearly every day, and when he arrived late again that day the boss fired him. His mother had gone out of town for the week, and in her absence he had gone on a spree of alcohol and drug use that left him in no condition to work each morning. He had taken "uppers" until late at night, "downers" to make him sleep, then "uppers" to get him up again. The result was that "I would get too screwed up and then I'd sleep past the time I was supposed to wake up."

By "downers," he explained, he meant alcohol and marijuana; the "upper" he used was cocaine. He seemed to recognize that he had a problem controlling his substance use, although he did not see himself as being dependent on drugs. "I don't feel that I have a drug addiction problem," he said. "I just feel I have a problem with trying to control myself, of when I'm going to do it and when I'm not."

He had come to rely on the drugs to relax him and help him unwind.

The downer before the bedtime is just kind of a nice thing for me to sit back and enjoy. [What kind of feeling does it induce?] *It induces*

151

the feeling of complete relaxation, and you can deal with your problems when you wake up. [Do you like to feel that way before you go to bed?] *Yeah. I like to feel completely relaxed. . . . I enjoy it because it seriously relieves my stress.*

As in his working life, his personal relationships were in serious disorder. His relationships with both of his parents had been badly damaged by their divorce about a year ago. His description illustrates the way children often find themselves beleaguered emotionally in the aftermath of their parents' divorce:

They never got along and they got divorced about a year ago. They still aren't getting along. . . . Ever since then, my dad's been in a really bad depression . . . he's real bad. And my mom's kind of on the wigged-out side right now. She's trying to get her life pulled back together. . . . So I get caught in the middle because my mom will nag nag nag to me, and then my dad will be like "I'm so depressed. This is going wrong and this is going wrong," and I'm like "Dad, I can't help you."

He had a girlfriend until recently, but they broke up. The experience had soured him on romance for a long time to come. "I was living with her for about eight months; oh man, that was hell," he said. "After it was over, I decided that was it; I don't want a relationship right now. . . . I haven't gone out with anyone steady since then, and I really don't want to either. Now, when I'm forty or something, maybe I can do it again." What made the experience so unpleasant for him was the way he felt she tried to restrict him. "I'm eighteen years old, and I've got better things to do than listen to somebody who's going to nag nag nag about every little thing you do." For example, she expected him to go to bed at the same time she did and became angry when he would not.

His sense of chafing under the restrictions that others imposed on him was a theme that came up often in the interview. It was one of the reasons he disliked school. "It was very aggravating to me because I didn't like people saying 'This is it, and this is what you're going to do.'" His relationship with his parents had been high in conflict earlier in his teens because of the rules they attempted to impose. They did not like his earring, or his long hair, or the way he was drifting from one job to another. His relationship with his father had been especially troubled. "My dad, when

I first got my ear pierced and started letting my hair grow out, he really ragged on me; he came down real hard on me. . . . I would go through jobs once a week or something, and he got real disappointed with that and he ragged on me real bad for it. . . . For a while, we wouldn't talk, we didn't like each other."

He also saw his older sister as attempting to oppress him. "She just doesn't approve of anything I do," he said. "Nothing at all. She sits there and says 'The only reason I'm saying this is because I care about you,' and I said, 'If you have the littlest feeling of care in your body for me, you would not sit there and rag on me all the time.' Her ragging on me, it's not her trying to guide me; it's her ragging on me."

When he talked about religion, too, the theme of intolerable restriction on his self-expression emerged.

Maybe there is a god, but I feel I cannot sit here on this earth and live my life by him because I'd feel I'd miss out on so much. If I started being religious, I just have a feeling it would take away a lot of the stuff that I feel happy and comfortable with. I feel like it would control my life. If you start going to church and you start listening, they're saying "This is a sin and this is a sin and this is a sin." You know, "premarital sex is a sin. Going out and having a good time drinking under age is a sin." Just all kinds of stuff is a sin, but all that stuff I enjoy, and it would just take all that away. . . . If there is a god, I don't feel that he would want to restrict all that from me. Because that's basically almost a miserable life.

He saw heavy metal songs as expressions of his own views on the desirability of living a highly individualized life. "I think what they're doing with heavy metal is, they're making a voice. And I think it's just saying 'Don't be like everybody else. There's ways to be different and still live.'" The songs reinforced and legitimized his resistance to the pressure he felt from others to comply with social conventions. "Heavy metal is kind of a way for me to sit down and say 'Well, I'm not the only one fighting back.'"

Barry had numerous difficulties in love and work, but he saw the problems of his life as extending entirely from others' attempts to restrain him rather than from his own incapacity for self-restraint. He had arrived on the threshold of adulthood dangerously ill-equipped for the kind of self-regulation and future planning required for most kinds of adult success. Even for his fervently held dream of becoming a heavy metal star, he was reluctant to make any kind of systematic plan.

[What do you see yourself doing in ten years?] *I don't really like to live for the future. I like to live "Here I am today." I would really enjoy moving out to L.A. or Boston and being in a heavy metal band. I would really like to do that, but I'm not going to set too many goals because right now, I'm here today, and I may die tonight or something. So I've got to just go out and do what I've got to do today. I do look into the future somewhat because I know that it will get here maybe eventually, but I just don't plan on it.*

Summary profile: Barry

Age: 18
Race: White
Education: dropped out in 9th grade
Current occupation: framer (at photography store)
Father's occupation: manager, soft drink bottling company
Mother's occupation: real estate property manager
Family background: adopted when six weeks old, parents divorced one year ago
Spent most of childhood in: Atlanta
Number of heavy metal recordings owned: 250–300
Favorite heavy metal groups: Dokken
Goals in ten years: play in heavy metal band, or own construction company
Political orientation: "pissed off"
Religious orientation: atheist
Hobbies/leisure preferences: playing guitar
Number of times in past year:

Driven a car under the influence of alcohol:	2–5
Driven a car over 80 miles per hour:	>50
Driven a car greater than 20 mph over speed limit:	>50
Had sex without contraception:	>10
Had sex with someone not known well:	2–5
Used marijuana:	>10
Used cocaine:	>10
Damaged or destroyed public or private property:	0
Shoplifted:	6–10

Heavy Metal Music, Individualism, and Adolescent Alienation

This book has focused on the lives of American adolescent boys, and the portrait of adolescent life presented in the previous chapters is likely to disturb anyone who cares deeply about adolescents, indeed anyone who cares deeply about the current and future state of American society. There are millions of adolescent heavy metal fans in the United States, and there may be millions of other adolescents who do not care for the music but who sympathize with the ideology of alienation. Heavy metal fans (such as the adolescents described in the previous chapters) are an extreme group, but they provide stark and startling examples of sentiments shared, to some degree, by many American adolescents. As we have seen, many of them are profoundly alienated from the institutions that have formed the bedrock of American society for over 200 years: from their families, from their schools, from their communities, and from political and religious institutions. Perhaps their one salient connection to their culture is that they share the cultural belief system of individualism—but they take it to such an extreme that it becomes hyperindividualism[1] and another facet of their alienation.

Such profound and pervasive alienation among many American adolescents suggests that the process of socializing them into their culture has failed in serious ways. When socialization works, it leads children to embrace the ways of their culture so that, by the end of adolescence, they consider the ways of their culture to be their own ways.[2] When it works their culture becomes the prism though which experience enters their hearts and minds; it helps them organize their experience and give it coherence and meaning. Alienation is a sign that it has not worked, that they consider the ways of their culture to be alien to their personal identities, that they have rejected the prism for understanding life that their culture has held out to them.

This is a precarious state for adolescents to be in as they stand at the threshold of adulthood, preparing to enter an adult society they do not respect and do not really consider to be their own. In this chapter we examine the consequences of individualistic socialization for adolescents reaching the transition to adulthood.

The ultimate source of alienation

In previous chapters we have explored a variety of sources of adolescent alienation, including damaged or absent ties to family, community, school, and religion. Heavy metal music has been discussed mostly as a reflection and expression of their alienation, although it is also true that heavy metal music, and the heavy metal subculture many adolescents are part of, legitimizes their alienation and in doing so may reinforce and strengthen it. But even if there were no heavy metal at all, adolescent alienation in American society would still exist in formidable proportions. If heavy metal did not exist, adolescents would have to invent it, or some comparable way of declaring their alienation.

Far more important than heavy metal music, as a source of adolescent alienation, is our cultural ideology of individualism, which has had consequences that its original proponents did not intend and most of its contemporary proponents do not even realize. In its original form individualism was conceived as a liberation of individuals from the oppressive restrictions of the state, particularly restrictions on how they might practice religion. Arguably the American experiment with individualism succeeded admirably in the seventeenth, eighteenth, and nineteenth centuries, for those able to take advantage of the liberties it offered.[3] The country thrived and expanded, and people immigrated to the United States from all over the world, many of them drawn by the promise of greater individual freedoms.

However, individualism also thrived and expanded during this time, and freedom from state coercion became freedom from religious coercion, which in turn became freedom from religious obligations, then freedom from obligations to community and even to family. If individualism was a good thing, the reasoning seemed to run, then more of it must be even better. In the twentieth century, and particularly after World War II, individualism swung to an extreme of hyperindividualism. The cultural ideal became the person who could completely ignore social influences, whether from the government, organized religion, the community, or the family, and live a life of unrestrained independence and self-expression.

This remains the American cultural ideal,[4] even though the problems in American society—particularly in the lives of adolescents—have mounted during the half-century hyperindividualism has risen to dominance. Although many people from all quarters of American life would agree that adolescent alienation and related problems have increased dramatically during this time, fewer see a cultural ideal of hyperindividualism as the ultimate source of the problems. Instead, the causes cited range from poor job prospects for adolescents as they enter adulthood, to the breakdown of the family, to heavy metal music and other media. There are even those who claim that adolescent alienation in our time results from *too much* adult involvement in the lives of adolescents rather than too little, that is, from *not enough* free rein for adolescent self-expression.[5]

I disagree, of course, and I think the simplest and clearest test of the different views is in cross-cultural and historical comparisons. As the cultural comparisons presented in the previous chapters have shown, many other cultures are far more narrow in their socialization than we are, guiding the development of adolescents far more carefully and tightly than we do. Yet they have less adolescent alienation and fewer adolescent problems, not more.[6] Similarly, few people will dispute that within American society socialization has broadened over the past half-century and that there are fewer adult-directed demands and restrictions on adolescents now than before. Yet adolescent alienation has burgeoned during this time, and adolescent problems have escalated, not diminished.

Perhaps one reason we have failed to recognize individualism as the ultimate source of adolescent alienation is that not all of the consequences of individualism, even hyperindividualism, are negative ones; some of the consequences are in fact highly desirable. Individualism encourages individual development in a way that, for some, brings out individual talents and allows them to express themselves in ways that are creative and original. We have seen some of these benefits in the previous chapters, in the lives of boys who have formed creative, thoughtful ideas about politics and religion and who are pursuing unusual career paths. Recall Reggie's vigorous and witty defense of his religious skepticism. Recall the prospective career paths of some of the other boys profiled: Mark, who hopes to become a marine biologist and work for Greenpeace, or Lew, who wants to create a horror opera blending heavy metal and theater. However, even as we appreciate the creativity that individualism allows, we should not overlook the cost it exacts in the lives of many adolescents: profound alienation, loneliness, a sense of disconnection from all others, and a potentially problematic transition to adulthood. Below, we consider the consequences of individualism for adolescents' transition to adulthood, focusing on consequences with regard to the three goals of socialization introduced in Chapter 2: self-regulation, preparation for adult roles, and providing sources of meaning.

Consequences of individualism: Self-regulation and preparation for adult roles

By the time of the transition to adulthood the goals of self-regulation and preparation for adult roles are intimately related because the capacity for self-regulation, for impulse control, is required for the performance of adult roles. Even the American majority culture, with its cultural belief system of individualism, has certain norms and expectations for adult roles that require people to modify their individualism to some degree. This is because norms and expectations of some kind are inherent in adult roles. By definition, filling a role means trimming your impulses to some extent, in order to conform to the requirements inherent in the role. The two key areas of adult roles in every culture are *love* and *work*,[7] and both inevitably require limitations on the egoistic desires of the individual. The implication of this is that socialization according to a belief system of individualism may be misguided. Or perhaps it would be more accurate to say that though it works well for many, it has failed for young people of the kind we have been listening to throughout this book. For such young people, socialization that exalts an extreme form of individualism brings them into adulthood without the self-regulation that is necessary to perform adult roles successfully.

In love, taking the role of a partner in an intimate love relationship requires the capacity to limit your sexual impulses and focus them on a particular person.[8] It also requires limiting your egoism, particularly if you and the other person live in the same household. There are many small decisions to be made in the course of daily living, and successful partners learn to compromise and sacrifice on behalf of one another, with the trust that the compromises and sacrifices will be mutual and will contribute to the long-term happiness of them both. If one or both partners refuse to limit their own desires for the sake of the other, the relationship is unlikely to survive for long. However, some of the children raised in a culture that exalts individualism may be ill-prepared for such limitations when they reach adulthood, even if observing those limitations would promote their own long-term interests.

Among the boys I interviewed for the study, it was remarkable how few of them had a steady girlfriend. No more than a handful had a gratifying and enduring relationship with a young woman. In some cases, for example in the case of Barry, whose profile precedes this chapter, it was clear that this was at least partly due to a reluctance to make the kinds of compromises necessary for living together in an equal relationship (even the simple compromise of when to go to sleep).

The problem is not that they are not loving. They are capable of the strongest attachments; many of them have a good relationship with at least one parent, usually the mother, and nearly all of them have at least one close friend. However, their love relationships are most successful when the attachment is to someone who makes few or no demands on them. Parents are most likely to be loved and admired when they allow the boys to do whatever they like, without restraint. Friends, too, are valued for the unconditional acceptance they offer. Potential love partners outside the family are unlikely to provide the same degree of freedom.

Erik Erikson argued that learning the role of partner in a love relationship is crucial to development in young adulthood. Erikson described a central challenge for each part of a person's life, and in young adulthood the challenge is one of *intimacy versus isolation.*[9] Young adulthood should be a time when a person forms a stable, intimate relationship with another person, outside the family of origin. The alternative, when this challenge is not met successfully, is isolation. The isolation of many of the boys in this study is vivid—consider the cases of Jack, who at eighteen trusted no one; and Lew, who had no friends even among fellow metalheads—and there is a danger that it may increase as they move into young adulthood. Friendships may prove to be harder to find and sustain as previous friends form intimate relationships; young adults incapable of intimacy may find themselves left behind, deepening further their alienation. The freedom promised by individualism may be a meager consolation by then.

In work, too, role performance requires the capacity for self-regulation and the limitation of desire, qualities not cultivated in socialization that is highly individualistic. Most occupations involve a hierarchy of relationships where virtually every person involved is subordinate to at least one other person. Self-regulation is required in any hierarchy, because it enables people to comply with demands from those higher up even when they would prefer not to. Self-regulation also means refraining from pleasures that interfere with the capacity to work. Recall Spencer, who lost his job because of a wild drunken adventure the night before he was to drive a moving van across the country, and Barry, who lost his job because his drug use caused him to oversleep on several consecutive mornings.

Work also requires self-regulation in the sense that there are few occupations that do not involve at least some tasks that are mundane or disagreeable. However, most metalheads are high-sensation seekers whose socialization has not provided them with constructive ways to control and direct their sensation-seeking desires. As a result, most typical jobs strike them as a grim prospect. They demand something far more exciting and interesting than exists in most of the jobs likely to be available to them.

In one sense this is refreshing. The occupations they aspire to are original, dynamic, and out of the ordinary, almost without exception: CIA

A stage diver plunges in. (Photo by Nick Romanenko)

agent, writer, airplane pilot, actor—and, of course, heavy metal star. There is an inclination to admire them and wish them well in the pursuit of their youthful dreams. However, a troubling question soon asserts itself: How will they react when their dreams clash with reality and they are forced to accept an occupation far less appealing to them than the life of a heavy metal star? Durkheim's warning rises again: that young people whose expectations for life are inflated beyond the capacity of the world to match them are in danger of becoming deeply alienated from the adult society they will soon be entering, with dire consequences for their own well-being and for the fate of their society. For the metalheads, whose heavy metal dreams are one of the few flames blazing now in the darkness of their alienation, the prospect that those flames will be extinguished in the years to come, thus deepening further their already profound alienation, is chilling indeed.

Consequences of individualism: Sources of meaning

In addition to teaching self-regulation and preparing young people for the requirements of adult roles, socialization typically provides the members of a culture with common sources of meaning. Human beings have an existential dilemma that other animals do not have. We know we will die one day, and we want to know what the significance of a human life is in light of human mortality.[10] Human beings truly cannot live "by bread alone"—we want to understand the larger significance of life; we want to know the *meaning* of it.

Through socialization, cultures provide their members with sources of meaning. Typically this includes some kind of religious belief system that provides answers to vexing questions about the ultimate source of all life and the ultimate destination of the soul. However, sources of meaning are not limited to religious beliefs. They also include attachments to family, community, and perhaps tribe, nation, or other large groups. By identifying with these groups and developing a sense of interdependence with fellow members, people gain a sense of being a part of something that began before they were born and will endure after they have gone. They also gain, in the present, a sense of mutual emotional security and support with fellow group members.

We have seen, in some detail, how little religious beliefs mean to many American adolescents. The Judeo-Christian beliefs of generations past seem remote to them, like a story one might find in a children's book but that no sensible person would actually believe. Often, organized religion is not merely irrelevant to them, it is an irritant, seen as a bastion of corruption and hypocrisy, a threat to unbridled individualism. Individualism itself is the foundation of their belief system, the prism through which they make sense of things. But individualism does not provide answers to many of the most vexing existential questions. It simply says, "Find your own."

The other sources of meaning common to many cultures—the interdependencies and attachments to others that most cultures provide—are also weak in American society. As we have seen, for many adolescents ties to others are few and are often problematic. A large portion of their alienation is simply loneliness; they are aware of the lack of meaningful attachments in their lives, and they suffer from it. One study indicates that American adolescents spend about 25 percent of their time alone, much of it brooding over their loneliness.[11]

Their sources of meaning in relation to others are lacking in another way, more subtle but perhaps more serious. Many of them make no important contributions to their families or communities. Although the majority of American adolescents are employed, the income from this employment typically goes toward themselves and their leisure activities. They contribute little or nothing to common enterprises. In contrast, such contributions are a key source of meaning in most other cultures. One of the things that is evident from cross-cultural studies of child development is how children in most cultures make important contributions to their families from the time they are quite young.[12] This requires little coercion on the part of parents; for the most part, children are eager to learn how to do what adults and "big kids" are doing. From the time they are just toddlers, when they can barely walk and barely speak, they are modeling themselves after the behavior of adults and trying to involve themselves in their work. In fact, "play" for children in most cultures does not involve specially designed children's toys that have no connection to adult life, but some junior version of adult work—"playing house," or working the ground with a child-sized hoe.

By the time children in these cultures have reached even age eight or nine they are contributing important work to the family. There is a great sense of satisfaction, for these children, in being able to perform an important role in the family, and their involvement in this work cultivates in them a sense of their responsibilities and mutual obligations to the other family members. By the time they reach adolescence their socialization has made interdependence, not independence, the primary value by which they live their daily lives, and their contribution to their families has become a central and reliable source of meaning.

Adolescents in the United States spend far less time on household work than adolescents in other cultures.[13] American parents like to feel that by requiring little or nothing from their adolescents in the way of family responsibilities, they are respecting their individuality and treating them as near-equals, as the psychologists recommend. It is the conventional wisdom in psychology that parents should treat children in their midteens as near-adults, as peers. This might indeed be good advice, if it meant requiring adult-like responsibilities out of them. In practice, however, most often it means requiring virtually nothing out of them. This is hardly treating them as adults, or equals. What parent would tolerate another adult in the household who contributed little in either money or labor? On the contrary, adolescents in many American households are treated not like equal adults but like indulged guests.

This is not a healthy arrangement, either for adolescents or their families. Having few responsibilities leaves them isolated and disconnected from the family and deprives them of an important source of meaning. In addition, it leaves them with little appreciation of the work that other family members contribute. It may also give them the sense that they are entitled to indulgence and that any requirement to contribute something to the household constitutes intolerable oppression.

A recent study of how adolescents spend their time provides interesting insights into the distribution of household duties among adolescents and their parents.[14] Family members carried beepers around and were signaled at random times during the day, at which points they would record what they were doing, with whom, their mood at the moment, and other reflections. One notable conclusion of the study was that adolescents contribute very little of their time toward the household—far less than their fathers or (especially) their mothers, even when both parents work full time. Of the time adolescents spend at home, virtually all of it is spent on themselves, in grooming, listening to music, watching TV, and chatting on the phone. Furthermore, on the rare occasions when the beeper found them doing household work, it also found them in a foul mood. Being required to contribute work to the household seemed to irritate them tremendously. The authors concluded that "many of these adolescents, especially boys, felt little responsibility for their family's needs, and were therefore annoyed when asked to do their part" (pp. 99–100). Among the metalheads, recall how Rich taunted and defied his father when he was asked to mow the lawn. Small wonder that parents of adolescents often find it easier simply to do the tasks themselves than to struggle to persuade their adolescents to do them.

Although American adolescents often complain and resist when their parents attempt to persuade them to make even a modest contribution to the household, this is not an inevitable consequence of asking adolescents to contribute work. There is nothing inherent in adolescent development that means they should naturally resist involvement in adult tasks, in spite of our cultural myths about the inevitability of adolescent rebelliousness. On the contrary, their resistance is the culmination of many years of a particular kind of cultural socialization, which is broad to the point of permissiveness. We know from observations around the world that there are many cultures in which adolescents do indeed reach near-adult status in work, and work alongside adults. There is no obstacle, in their intellectual or physical development, that would prevent adolescents from performing most work by the time they are in their late teens. In these cultures adolescent girls become nearly as adept as their mothers at caring for children and running a household; adolescent boys become nearly as adept as their fathers at cultivating crops, or hunting, or fishing, or whatever work it is that sustains the economy and is the basis for survival.[15]

The kind of skills required for adult work in an information-based economy like that of the United States (and other postindustrial economies) take longer to acquire, and adolescents have not yet accumulated the knowledge required to perform many adult jobs. However, there is no reason why adolescents could not, and should not, do adult-like work within the family. Adolescents are certainly capable of caring for younger children, planning and preparing meals, keeping a household clean, and the other myriad tasks that are part of modern adult life. For adolescents who are employed, there is no reason why they could not commit part of their income toward the family. When adolescents do not contribute to the family in American households, it is not because they cannot; it is because we will not teach them to value it and will not require it of them.

American parents mean well, of course, in excusing adolescent children from the obligations of family life, but they may actually be doing their children a great disservice. This is not meant to blame the parents. As I explained in Chapter 2, parents in all cultures draw their parenting practices from their cultures. Furthermore, parents are only one source among many in their adolescents' socialization. The cultural belief system of individualism pervades not only socialization in the family but also schools, communities, and the media. We have seen, in these pages, examples of the futile efforts of parents who attempt to swim against the cultural tide of individualism but find their efforts swept under by it. However, most parents swim with rather than against the cultural tide of socialization, and for American parents, including the parents of most of the boys in this study, this means promoting their children's independence and individualism to the greatest extent possible. The consequence of this kind of socialization is not only pervasive self-centeredness among adolescents, but, for some, profound alienation. Ironically, although American parents intend to promote their children's self-esteem by encouraging their independence from the family and making few demands on them for contributions to the family, the effect is sometimes the opposite of what they intended: Rather than gaining self-esteem, adolescents may suspect they are not useful or important anywhere, even in their own families.

Some of them turn to heavy metal music as an alternative source of meaning and as an expression of the dearth of meaning in their lives. In Chapter 1 I discussed the significance of the heavy metal concert as a "manhood ritual" in the sense that, like other manhood rituals around the world, it contains elements of music, high-sensation intensity, physical strenuousness, and the celebration of common values and a common view of life. However, as I also noted, the heavy metal concert differs crucially from other manhood rituals in that it is not structured and directed by adults whose interest is in inducing the adolescents to accept and embrace the values and norms of their culture. On the contrary, the metalheads' participation in the heavy metal concert and the heavy metal subculture more generally leads them to reject rather than embrace adult values and norms.

This is a consolation to them in their adolescence, and it is an important source of meaning. They feel alienated, estranged from their culture, but heavy metal turns alienation into a defiant celebration. There is a paradox here: The American majority culture exalts individualism, and yet the metalheads, who also exalt individualism, reject that culture and feel alienated from it. The explanation for this is that many of the metalheads,

From the mouths of metalheads comes an alarm. . . . (Photo by Nick Romanenko)

having grown up in such a culture, experience any restraint whatsoever as intolerable. Even an individualistic culture has certain norms and rules for behavior; otherwise there would be a complete collapse of social order. However, the metalheads, as well as many other adolescents growing up in the contemporary West, find even these minimal restrictions to be oppressive and unjust. It is a fulfillment of Durkheim's prophecy: For people who fail to develop the capacity for self-regulation, no amount of unrestraint will satisfy them. Reality itself appears as the last intolerable restraint, because their expectations become so high that nothing in the real world can match it. Alienation is the inevitable result.

Heavy metal gives expression to their alienation, but ultimately it is unlikely to prove reliable as a source of meaning. It might be tempting to compare the heavy metal subculture, historically and cross-culturally, to other movements that have been forces for constructive social change. One could cite numerous examples of adolescents being unhappy with the status quo of society, critical of the adults who possess the primary authority and power, and contemptuous of the hypocrisy and compromise of principle that often accompany the exercise of power in political and religious institutions. It is often the young people, adolescents and young adults, who provide the energy and take the risks that bring about social change. In recent history one thinks of the youthful Czech protesters in Wenceslas Square in 1989; some lost their lives beneath tanks sent to squelch the protest, but the protesters' efforts soon prevailed. Also fresh in the world's memory are the demonstrations that same year in Tiananmen Square in China, when youthful students took similar risks and were brutally suppressed.

In a sense, the themes in heavy metal songs are simply a contemporary expression of this adolescent capacity for energetic and righteous social criticism. However, what distinguishes the heavy metal ideology from other such protests is its deep cynicism. Typically, social criticism includes an aspiration for change and a prescription for improvement. Heavy metal has no such aspiration and no such prescription. The world has been hopelessly ruined, the message goes. Forget about improving or re-creating family, school, community, or religious ideals—none of them can be trusted. All that is left to you is to seek some kind of consolation and refuge, on your own.

The future of adolescent alienation

We may now have found ourselves nearing a point where American individualism has "grown cancerous," in the words of Robert Bellah and his colleagues.[16] Until recently that individualism was held in check by ties to family, community, religion, and nation. A healthy tension existed between the two, with individualism preventing the social ties from becoming oppressive and the social ties preventing the individualism from becoming irresponsible or resulting in alienation. However, these ties have become frayed for a large proportion of American society over the past fifty years, even snapping altogether for many people. Heavy metal is the specter of this decline in social ties. From the mouths of metalheads comes an alarm, a warning of deepening and widening decline to come if nothing is done to change the culture's course away from ever more radical individualism.

Is there a remedy for adolescent alienation? As I have indicated, one strategy is for parents to involve children in the common family life, to cultivate a sense of mutual obligation and responsibility from early on. This would culminate in treating adolescents as near-equal members of the household—not just with near-equal rights but with near-equal responsibilities as well. Parents cannot expect to succeed in this if they wait until children reach puberty. The sense of family interdependence must be cultivated from the time children are young, and it must become a source of meaning with the years. Still, the heavy metal subculture and the hyperindividualism that it reflects are part of a larger cultural pattern, and even the best efforts of parents may be erased by sources of socialization that invite adolescents to expand their individualism without restraint.

However, there is reason for some optimism that the momentum toward hyperindividualism will be modified into something less selfish and less alienating as the contemporary children of this culture grow up. Adolescents grow ineluctably into adulthood, and, as noted, adult roles inherently hold demands that require people to modify their individualism. As the adolescents described here take on adult roles in love and work, many of them will develop, by necessity, the capacity for self-regulation that has been missing in them up to now. Socialization continues beyond childhood and adolescence; adults also change and grow and responding to socialization influences. There is a danger that adolescents of the kind we have met in this book will be unable to adapt to the requirements of adult roles and become even more seriously alienated. However, many of them will eventually make the necessary adaptations, even if it takes them until their late twenties or even their thirties to do so.

The other saving grace of a hyperindividualist culture, in the long run, is likely to be the human need for emotional ties to others. We are born into the world in need of attachments to others; without such attachments, something as vulnerable as a human infant would never survive. This need is the basis of human social relationships, and it is something all of us take into adulthood. Although it may be eroded or damaged by the time we get there, it keeps us seeking the security, comfort, satisfaction, and meaning that potentially exist in social ties. Over the past fifty years, and to a less radical extent for 300 years before that time, we have been stampeding toward the allurements of freedom *from* social ties. We have been drawn in this direction because of the restrictiveness and oppression social ties sometimes bring, and because of the seductiveness of the abstract idea of unbridled individualism. However, there is some evidence of a growing cultural awareness that we have reached the outer extreme of individualism, where it becomes a corrosive hyperindividualism, and that along the way we have unwittingly shed much that was valuable. Critics of individualism such as Robert Bellah, Amitai Etzioni, and Christopher Lasch have found a large and receptive audience. Perhaps this awareness will, in turn, lead us back from that extreme, in pursuit of restoring social ties and of reconstructing them for our time.

It remains necessary to articulate the costs of hyperindividualism, in order to bring to broader awareness what is lost if society is made up of atomistic individuals who care little for anything beyond themselves. The pervasive and dominating themes of this culture—that self-love is a virtue rather than something to be overcome, that self-esteem is always superior to self-restraint or self-denial—deserve to be challenged. Clear and contemporary alternatives to hyperindividualism should be stated and offered. For those who wish to promote such alternatives, heavy metal music provides the useful function of giving them some idea of what they are up against. The heavy metal blend of alienation and hyper-individualism is powerful, and it has the allegiance of millions of American adolescents. These adolescents will soon become a significant proportion of American adults, and they may retain their alienation and cynicism even if they relinquish their affection for the high-sensation barrage of sound that is heavy metal. The challenge for those who are disturbed by the message of heavy metal is to provide other voices, voices that will prove as compelling an argument for mutual obligation, social responsibility, and interdependence as heavy metal has shown itself to be for alienated individualism.

appendix: interview questions

1. How many recordings (album, cassette, CD) do you have by heavy metal (HM) groups?

2. What percentage of your total collection is HM? What other kinds of music do you have/like/listen to?

3. What do you like about heavy metal? Why do you listen to it?

4. Give me some examples of groups you like. Why do you like these groups?

5. Give me some examples of songs you especially like. Why do you like these songs, and what are they about?

6. Do you pay more attention to the lyrics or to the music?

7. Is there a typical volume that you play it at?

8. How many concerts have you been to in the last year? Which groups?

9. What do you wear, typically, when you go to a concert? Do you dress differently for the concert than at other times?

10. Tell me about one of the concerts you went to. What was it like, what did you do before and after, etc.

11. Who do you usually go with? The same group every time? Boys and girls together, or just one or the other?

12. At a concert, have you ever moshed/slamdanced? If yes, why, and what is it like?

13. Do you have a boyfriend/girlfriend/someone you date regularly? If yes, how long have you been seeing each other? What's the longest you ever dated someone? Do you go to concerts with them? Do they also like this kind of music? Do you prefer boys/girls who like HM?

14. How much would you say you spend per month on things related to HM— cassettes, CDs, albums, t-shirts, magazines, concert tickets?

15. What do your parents think of HM? Do they approve or disapprove? Do they criticize you for playing it when you're home together?

16. Are your parents divorced? If divorced: how old were you when they divorced? What was it like for you? How often do you see (noncustodial parent)?

17. More about your parents: how would you say you get along with them? What issues do you argue about?

18. Do you have brothers and sisters? (Include ages.) Do they like heavy metal?

19. Where were you born? How many times has your family moved since you were born? Have the moves been good for you or bad for you?

20. How long have you liked HM? How did you first get interested in it?

21. Do you listen to HM more when you're in a certain kind of mood? Does it put you in any particular mood?

22. What do you see yourself doing in ten years?

23. How would you describe yourself politically? Are there any particular issues that are especially important to you?

24. How would you describe yourself religiously? How often do you go to church or temple?

25. Some people say that there are a lot of satanic messages in HM music. Do you think so?

26. How do you like school? What classes do you like best? Least?

27. Do you get involved in school activities—choir, student government, going to football and basketball games, that kind of thing? Do you have other hobbies, interests?

28. Do most of your friends also like this kind of music? Do you listen to it together, lend each other recordings, etc.?

29. Name three people you admire.

30. Do you play a musical instrument? If yes: what kind of music? In a band?

31. What's the most reckless/wild/dangerous thing you've ever done? Describe the episode.

notes

Preface

1. I interviewed 48 of the boys and collected questionnaires from another 22 male heavy metal fans in the course of collecting the data for the comparison group. These 22 were boys who indicated on a questionnaire of musical preferences that they "strongly liked" heavy metal music. Similarly, with the female fans, 25 were interviewed and information on 13 others (who "strongly liked" heavy metal) was obtained in the course of collecting data for the comparison group.

The data obtained through the volunteer/interview method and the classroom survey method were highly similar. That is, with few exceptions, the differences between the metalheads and other boys that are reported in the following chapters were statistically significant whether the nonmetalheads were compared to the volunteer/interview group, to metalheads surveyed in the classroom, or to both combined.

2. The mean ages for the comparison groups were 16.9 for boys and 17.7 for the girls. Walser (1993) presents survey data indicating that nearly all heavy metal fans are in the 13- to 25-year-old age range. There was one exception in my sample, an unusual 31-year-old man, but I did not include him in the analysis because his age was so much different (for a profile of him, see Arnett, 1993).

3. I did not interview the adolescents in the comparison group; instead, I turned the questions that I had asked the metalheads in the interview into multiple-choice or open-ended items on a questionnaire for the comparison group, where they could write in their responses.

4. Walser (1993) claims that heavy metal fans are almost evenly divided between males and females, including at concerts. The reason for our divergence on this point is that he includes "glam metal" groups like Poison and Bon Jovi as heavy metal, whereas I do not (for reasons I explain in Chapter 3), and the audience for these groups is indeed roughly gender-balanced. For the heavy metal bands I include as metal, such as Judas Priest and Metallica, the audience is predominantly male, as I can attest from attending many of these concerts (and as Walser agrees). With regard to the age range, Walser (1993, p. 17) cites a 1984 survey indicating that two-thirds of heavy metal fans are 16–24 years old, with another one-fifth under 15 years old.

5. Arnett (1991a). In the high school sample, which does not include the boys who volunteered through the music store, 33 percent of boys indicated that they liked or strongly liked heavy metal, whereas only 16 percent of girls did.

6. Holinger and Offer (1989) show that the rate of suicide among adolescents in the United States has risen dramatically, by about 300 percent, over the past 30 years. But this increase has taken place almost entirely among white adolescent

boys. Among white girls and among black boys and girls, the rate has been nearly flat. As for automobile fatalities, the rate has risen sharply among adolescent boys over the past 50 years, rising only slightly among adolescent girls and actually *falling* among most other age/gender groups (Whitfield and Fife, 1987).

Chapter 1

1. See Hebdige (1979) and Brake (1985) on the ways that clothes and other elements of style declare membership in a youth subculture.

2. Walser (1993, ch. 4) describes heavy metal as providing the materials for building a distinctly male identity. Similarly, Weinstein (1991) notes that heavy metal "celebrates the very qualities that boys must sacrifice in order to become adult members of society" (p. 105).

3. Some academic observers—for example, Epstein and Pratto (1990), Weinstein (1991)—see this rejection as an admirable adolescent protest against an oppressive, "hegemonic" culture. I see it quite differently, as will become evident.

Part of their argument is that heavy metal represents a protest by working-class youth against the lack of economic opportunities available to them. See Gans (1974) and Hebdige (1979) for the general argument concerning class and mass-culture preferences, Weinstein (1991) and Walser (1993) for the argument specific to heavy metal. Weinstein makes this claim in her book but presents no data to support it. Walser (1993) concedes that heavy metal fans are as likely to be middle class as working class but nevertheless sees it as arising from the contradictions inherent in a capitalist society. In particular, he sees the violence and anger of heavy metal songs as a protest against the inadequate opportunities available to young people in our time and also as a protest against the injustices and depredations of capitalism. To me this requires quite a leap of interpretation, as very few heavy metal songs have anything to do with capitalism or with economic issues of any kind (see the song analysis in Chapter 3).

I do not think there is persuasive evidence for an argument based on social class. Heavy metal has millions of fans in the United States and around the world, and most evidence indicates that they are at least as likely to be middle class as working class. (See Lewis, 1987 for a summary of the evidence indicating that social class is only weakly related to musical preferences. Also, the data in Tanner, 1981 on Canadian adolescents showed heavy metal to be preferred equally by working-class and middle-class adolescents.) Among the metalheads I interviewed, few were from families where the father had an occupation that could be called working class (truck driver, factory worker); the majority were from middle- to upper-middle-class families (sons of insurance agents, electrical engineers, college professors, and so on). Also, even among the metalheads from working-class families, the sources of their alienation are rarely economic, as we shall see in Chapters 6 and 7. In fact, they often have exalted expectations for their own futures.

4. Gilmore (1991). The tasks of manhood I present here are outlined and detailed in this superb book.

5. Spencer (1965). See also Spencer (1973).

6. This argument is part of a theory I have developed on adolescent reckless behavior (Arnett, 1992a; 1992b). Here, my explanation of the boys' participation in the rituals departs from Gilmore (1991), who emphasizes the coercion necessary to get timid boys to participate. In contrast, I emphasize the alacrity of most boys to participate, as a consequence of the pleasure they take in high sensation.

7. James (1902/1961), pp. 289–290. It is important to note that James was writing in this way about war *before* the technologies of modern warfare were developed. None of his comments, or my use of his comments, is intended to apply to twentieth-century warfare, with its high-tech weaponry, atomic bombs, and cruise missiles.

8. Throughout this book I use the term "American majority culture." This term refers to the culture that is currently the dominant, majority culture that sets most of the norms and standards and holds most of the positions of political, economic, intellectual, and media power in this country. It is largely white and middle class, but most of the working class shares its values and way of life, and many non-white people in the middle class could also be considered part of the majority culture. I recognize that the United States contains other cultures that exist alongside the majority culture. These other cultures may be defined by racial, ethnic, religious, or other criteria, and they may have some similarities to the majority culture, but the term "American majority culture" is not intended to include them.

9. Sugerman (1991) ascribes the appeal of the hard rock band Guns N' Roses partly to the alienation of young people. Among the sources of alienation he cites is loss of meaningful ritual.

10. There are some exceptions to this, of course, in men who teach their sons how to use a gun or a rifle. But typically this is for hunting purposes, not to protect themselves and their families against human invaders.

11. True, we remain threatened (at least we did until the collapse of the Soviet Union) by intercontinental ballistic missiles, but protection from this threat is the province of only a tiny sector of the population. There is nothing most individuals can do about this threat and therefore no use including training in skills to protect us from it in the curriculum of socialization.

12. U.S. Department of Education (1988).

13. Arnett (1992a).

14. Jonah (1986).

15. Wilson and Herrnstein (1985).

16. For automobile driving, see Arnett (1992a; 1992b). For crime, see Katz (1982); see also Wilson and Herrnstein (1985, ch. 5), who suggest that many juvenile crimes are motivated by "sheer adventurousness" (p. 133), akin to a sensation-seeking motive.

17. Of course I am not suggesting that high sensation seeking is the *only* motivation for reckless driving or crime. Obviously, both are much more complicated than that, especially crime. But I am arguing that sensation seeking is a key motivation for these and other types of reckless behavior.

18. Zuckerman, Eysenck, and Eysenck (1978). There are weaknesses to their measure of sensation seeking, but it does compare people of different ages. I have also done such an age comparison, with a new measure of sensation seeking I

have developed (Arnett, 1994), and also found adolescents to be higher than adults in sensation seeking.

Chapter 2

1. Holinger and Offer (1989).
2. U.S. Dept. of Education (1988).
3. U.S. Dept. of Education (1988). Rates of drug use rose steadily through the 1970s before declining slightly in the 1980s.
4. Whitfield and Fife (1987).
5. Robinson, Buck, and Cuthbert (1991). This phenomenon has been described with regard to adolescents and popular music in this edited book.
6. For a more detailed presentation of the theory, see Arnett (1995a). The theory has also been applied to adolescent reckless behavior (Arnett, 1992a; 1992b; Arnett and Balle-Jensen, 1993) and the transition from adolescence to adulthood (Arnett and Taber, 1994).
7. See Spiro (1994, ch. 5).
8. For an example of this view, see Gaines (1991).
9. Roland (1988).
10. Larson and Richards (1994).
11. For an example, see Turnbull (1962).
12. Stevenson and Stigler (1992).
13. Linney and Seidman (1989); Stevenson and Stigler (1992).
14. Gilmore (1991).
15. Arnett (1995b).
16. Davis and Davis (1989).
17. It should be noted that this is not commanded as a joyless duty but as the believer's joyful submission to God and as the reliable path to true happiness.
18. Berger and Berger (1984).

Chapter 3

1. Weinstein (1991) and Walser (1993), in their books on heavy metal, included what I would call hard rock bands as metal bands, which is one of the reasons they reach somewhat different conclusions than I do about the nature and significance of heavy metal.
2. Music historians consider the first blues song to have been written by W. C. Handy in 1912.
3. Weinstein (1991), ch. 2.
4. See Weinstein (1991, ch. 2) for a chronology slightly different than the one offered here.
5. Weinstein (1991), ch. 2, p. 20.
6. Postman (1985) was referring to television, but it is no less true for music.
7. There are other ways to do this kind of analysis. I could have analyzed one album from each of 12 or 15 or 20 bands and included some relatively obscure bands (including some death metal) as well as the most prominent ones. How-

ever, I wanted to describe what *most* metalheads are listening to. For the most part, even metalheads who like the more obscure bands best also like and listen to at least some of the six bands included here.

8. Some readers may be concerned about a certain amount of tautological reasoning in this analysis: I defined heavy metal songs as songs with themes of alienation and anger, and then, voilà, discovered in my analysis that alienation and anger are prominent themes in heavy metal songs. But the purpose of the analysis is not so much to "prove" that heavy metal songs have these themes—as I said, these themes are partly what define heavy metal songs—but to look at the relative frequencies of various themes in the songs, including some such as substance abuse and suicide, which have been alleged to be a major part of the heavy metal genre but which, as I think this analysis demonstrates, are actually quite rare.

As Walser (1993) notes, one of the problems with other analyses of heavy metal songs is that they focus on the lyrics alone. Walser includes a complex musical analysis of particular songs in his book on heavy metal but surprisingly fails to note the pervasiveness of the use of minor keys in heavy metal songs, focusing instead on the use of particular musical modes rather than on the major/minor distinction. I would argue that whether the songs tend to be played in Phrygian mode or Aeolian mode is less significant *emotionally* and in its *meaning* than the simple fact that they tend to be in minor keys. The difference in our emphasis is partly because many of the songs he focuses on in his book are songs I would consider not heavy metal but hard rock, for example, songs by Van Halen, Deep Purple, Guns N' Roses, and Bon Jovi.

Oddly, although Walser emphasizes the importance of music over lyrics in the songs, his own analysis of 88 heavy metal songs uses the lyrics only (see chapter 5 of his book). He reports finding "relatively little concern with violence" in the songs (p. 139). The most common themes in his analysis are "assertion of or longing for intensity," lust, loneliness, love, and anger. However, his analysis includes songs from bands I consider hard rock and glam metal, not heavy metal. He agrees that songs by thrash metal bands such as Metallica "very often address violence, death, and madness in their lyrics" (p. 157).

9. This makes the analysis imperfect from a statistical point of view. Because some songs received only one lyrical category assignment while others received more than one, the songs that received more than one are overrepresented in the analysis. However, the alternative, of deciding on only one category for each song, seemed to me to sacrifice too much of the content of the songs—some songs really do have only one theme, others really do have more than one. So, although imperfect statistically, the analysis of lyrical themes can at least be taken as a rough sketch of the content of heavy metal songs.

10. Testimony of Dr. Joe Stuessy, U.S. Congress, *Record Labeling (Senate Hearing 99–529)*, 1985, p. 117. "[Heavy metal's] principal themes [include] substance abuse. . . ."

11. Robert Pielke (1986, p. 202), for example: "Most evident in heavy metal has been the attitude of negation, with its emphasis on the images of death, satanism, sexual aberration, dismemberment, and the grotesque." And Joe Stuessy: "Today's heavy metal is categorically different from previous forms of music. It contains the element of hatred, a meanness of spirit" (U.S. Congress, 1985, p. 117).

12. This song, like Ozzy's more recent "Demon Alcohol" quoted earlier in this chapter, is actually an anti-alcohol song. It begins like this: "Wine is fine but whiskey's quicker/ Suicide is slow with liquor." The lyrics do contain the phrase "suicide solution," and it's possible to imagine how an adolescent boy might have dwelled on that phrase to the exclusion of the rest of the lyrics. Nevertheless, defenders of Ozzy are right that it is ludicrous to hold him legally responsible for the boy's suicide. If this were valid, then no one should ever be allowed to publish a story, song, or factual account in which a person commits suicide. The fact is, even adolescent boys are not so easily manipulated. Literally millions of boys have listened to that song, and the fact that one of those boys killed himself shows nothing about the song as a "cause" of his suicide.

13. In an analysis of music videos, Kaplan (1987) reported that the theme of nihilism (which could be seen to be related to the angst theme here) is prominent in heavy metal videos.

14. For example, King (1988, p. 297): "The attraction of heavy metal music is its message that a higher power controls the world, and that power is hate—often personified by Satan."

15. Weinstein (1991), for example.

16. Fergusson (1961). In *Poetics*, it is tragedy in particular that Aristotle is discussing in this sense.

17. In my argument here I have drawn on Pattison's (1987) fine book, *The Triumph of Vulgarity: Rock Music in the Mirror of Romanticism*.

18. Aristotle discusses this as harmony and rhythm (Fergusson, 1961), but he is not using these terms in their musical sense. Rather, this refers to an aesthetically pleasing arrangement of parts in relation to the whole, so that the result is beautifully formed.

19. Although metalheads admire the musical expertise of the performers, the qualities named here tend to be more important than the *melodic* qualities of the music. The lack of importance of melody in heavy metal has been noted by Kaplan (1987), who described the music as "loud and unmelodious," filled with "relatively meaningless screaming sounds" (p. 107). Even Walser (1993), an ardent defender of the musical value of heavy metal songs, concedes that "melody is relatively less important in metal than in many other kinds of music" (p. 50).

20. See Hebdige (1979) for a discussion of how the offensive elements from subcultures that set themselves against society are eventually incorporated into the (widened) mainstream.

Chapter 4

1. This analogy is perhaps not as far-fetched as it may sound to some. Walser (1993, ch. 3) describes how many heavy metal guitarists have had classical training. In any case, my point here is that their *admiration* is similar to that of an admirer of classical music, not that Horowitz is comparable to the lead guitarist for Metallica or Megadeth.

2. Zuckerman, Eysenck, and Eysenck (1978). Zuckerman, who is most responsible for the conception and development of the sensation-seeking idea, emphasizes novelty and *complexity*. However, I think it is better defined by novelty and intensity, for reasons I explain in the paper presenting my own conception of sensation seeking and the scale of sensation seeking I have developed since the time I began this study (Arnett, 1994).

The sensation-seeking motive I describe here is analogous to the "intensity and power" that Walser (1993) reported as one of the main attractions of heavy metal according to the metalheads he surveyed. Interestingly, the other two factors he reported as important to metalheads also have parallels in my study: Musical skill was important to metalheads in both studies, and the truth and relevance of the lyrics reported by the metalheads he studied is similar to the ideology of alienation I describe below.

3. Arnett (1994); Zuckerman, Eysenck, and Eysenck, 1978.

4. In this study I used the *Sensation-Seeking Scale* by Zuckerman et al. (1978), as I had not yet developed my own scale. On this scale, metalheads were significantly higher in sensation seeking, compared to the other boys. For the items shown in Table 4.1, all differences are significant (in chi-square tests) at $p < .05$, and all but the one on parachute jumping are significant at $p < .01$.

5. Piaget (1967).

Chapter 5

1. In a statistical analysis of the types of behavior in Table 5.1, the metalheads were significantly higher than the other boys on every type of reckless behavior considered. The statistical analyses were conducted with the reckless behaviors as continuous variables (not dichotomous, as shown in the table), with structured responses. For most variables, the response categories were: 0, 1, 2–5, 6–10, more than 10 (times in past year). For the high-speed driving variables, the categories were: 0, 1–5, 6–10, 11–20, 21–50, and more than 50. See Arnett (1991a) for a detailed analysis.

In a related finding, Epstein et al. (1990) reported that, among boys attending a middle school for children with academic and/or behavior problems, 94 percent of the white boys stated that heavy metal was their favorite type of music (black boys preferred rap). The authors emphasized that, within the sample, there was not a significant relationship between musical preferences and behavior problems, but to me it is more notable that nearly all the boys at this school for children with serious problems preferred high-sensation, high-alienation music, that is, metal or rap.

2. For a more detailed statistical analysis of the relations between sensation-seeking, reckless behavior, and preference for heavy metal, see Arnett (1991a; 1992c). These analyses show sensation seeking to be related to every type of reckless behavior considered in the study; furthermore, the analyses support the interpretation that sensation seeking is the link between heavy metal music and reckless behavior.

3. U.S. Dept. of Education (1988).

4. Williams (1985).

5. See Feldman and Elliott (1990) for a commentary on the roles and responsibilities of contemporary Western adolescents.

6. These figures are, if anything, a low estimate of the extent to which they use the music for mood regulation. Many of them said they listen to heavy metal "all the time," and they were not counted in the proportion of those who listen to it especially when angry, even if they also listen to it when angry and gain emotional relief and release from it. See also Arnett (1991b).

7. This is a finding that is in line with the "uses-and-gratifications" tradition in media research (see Rubin, 1994, for a review), which arose as an antithesis to what were perceived as simplistic models of media effects. However, I do not think it is necessary to draw a sharp boundary between uses and effects; the catharsis experienced by the metalheads is both.

8. Kurdek (1987); Moore and Schultz, (1983). See also Gaines (1991) for some interesting examples of the cathartic effect of heavy metal.

9. Aristotle, writing almost 2,500 years ago in *Poetics*, was the first to use the term "catharsis" (Fergusson, 1961). However, he used the term in reference to art in general, and theatrical plays in particular, rather than applying it specifically to music.

10. There is an example of how the release of all this aggression at concerts may burst beyond the limits broadly defined by slamdancing and result in actual violence, but it involves Guns N' Roses, who are sometimes described as a heavy metal band but whose music is more similar to the bands I described as hard rock bands in Chapter 3. At a Guns N' Roses concert in July 1991, a riot broke out when Axl Rose, lead singer for the group, leaped into the crowd in pursuit of a fan who was annoying him by taking photographs. After security guards lifted him back onstage, Rose stalked off angrily and did not return. The fans proceeded to tear the theater apart, ripping out seats, throwing the speakers and other musical equipment from the stage to the ground, and battling police who descended upon the theater to restore order.

11. Elkind (1967; 1985); Arnett (1992a).

12. Elkind (1967; 1985).

13. Walser (1993) reported that over half the fans he surveyed at a Judas Priest concert said they played a musical instrument. See also Arnett (1991b).

14. Durkheim (1897/1951).

15. For more details, see Arnett (1992a; 1995a).

16. Wilson and Herrnstein (1985), chapters 4 and 5.

17. Udry (1988).

18. Durkheim's discussion of this in *Suicide* (1897/1951) is especially apt for heavy metal since the lyrics of the songs and the lives of the metalheads reflect alienation of the kind Durkheim discussed (using the term *anomie*).

Chapter 6

1. Perhaps the most impressive study in this area compared three groups of mothers in three different decades, raising their preschool children in 1940, in

1950, and in 1960 (Waters and Crandall, 1964). Over this twenty-year period, mothers became much less restrictive and less punitive, much more tolerant and more permissive. More recent studies of parenting attitudes indicate that most American parents, at least in the middle class, place independence and self-expression above obedience and conformity in the socialization of their children (Alwin, 1988; Alwin, Xu, and Carson, 1994; Kohn, 1977).

2. It should be noted that I interviewed only the boys and not their parents. Perhaps the picture of parenting that emerges from the boys' accounts would be somewhat different if the parents were also interviewed.

3. Numerous studies indicate that, following divorce, conflict is especially high between mothers and sons and that the adverse effects of divorce are stronger and more lasting for boys than for girls (Hetherington, 1991).

4. Hetherington (1991); Santrock et al. (1988).

5. See Demo and Aycock (1988) for a comprehensive review.

6. In order to examine family relationships, in addition to the interview questions I used the Family Relationships subscale of the Offer Self-Image Questionnaire (Offer, Ostrov, and Howard, 1982). Metalheads reported significantly poorer family relationships than other boys on the total scale (p < .01). Also, all of the item comparisons shown in Table 6.1 are significant at p < .05 or less.

7. These are the interconnections Bronfenbrenner (1979) describes as constituting the *mesosystem* of development.

8. Csikszentmihalyi and Larson (1984); Larson and Richards (1994).

9. Richards, Berk, and Forster (1979).

10. See Arnett (1995b) for a more detailed discussion of the role of media in adolescent socialization.

11. Herdt (1987). This traditional pattern has changed in the past decade with the introduction of primary school and other Western practices.

12. In their survey of children's development in cultures around the world, Whiting and Edwards (1988, ch. 2) note that children in most cultures have daily or near-daily contact with grandparents. The American middle class is the only exception they have observed. In a recent study of mine involving suburban American adolescents, only 25 percent of them reported living within 100 miles of their grandparents (Arnett and Jensen, 1994).

13. In the same study referred to in note 12 above, only 12 percent of adolescents said they saw their grandparents more than twenty times in the past year (Arnett and Jensen, 1994). I compared the American adolescents to Danish adolescents in this study; 90 percent of the Danish adolescents lived within 100 miles of their grandparents, and 37 percent saw their grandparents at least twenty times in the past year.

14. Postman (1985); Gober (1993).

15. Pitman and Bowen (1994).

16. In general, a distinction can be made between metalheads who are part of the "taste culture" of heavy metal and those who are part of the "subculture." A taste culture is a group of people who are united simply by a common entertainment preference—in this case heavy metal music. They have this musical preference in common, as well as the high sensation seeking that underlies it, but not much else. Members of the subculture are those for whom the music is something

more serious and essential, for whom the music is not just for fun but confirms an alternative value system and political/social ideology. For those in the subculture, an ideological convergence exists between them and the performers, in this case the ideology of alienation. Thus members of the taste culture share high sensation seeking, whereas members of the subculture share high sensation seeking plus alienation. There are boys from both the taste culture and the subculture among the metalheads I interviewed; wherever I discuss metalheads' alienation I have also sought to give examples of boys who simply like heavy metal as high-sensation music but who do not share the alienation. See Arnett (1993) and Lull (1987) for further discussion of this issue.

17. Durkheim (1897/1951), pp. 212, 214.

Chapter 7

1. See Karen Armstrong's excellent *A History of God* (1993). She notes that "there is a case for arguing that *Homo sapiens* is also *Homo religiosus*. Men and women started to worship gods as soon as they become recognizably human. . . . Indeed, our current secularism is an entirely new experiment, unprecedented in human history" (p. xix).

2. Much of the ensuing discussion is based on Stevenson and Stigler (1992).

3. Larson and Richards (1994).

4. Larson and Richards (1994), p. 88.

5. On this topic I did not ask a comparable question of the comparison group. However, an interesting comparison is to Glueck and Glueck's (1950) classic study of delinquents, where they found that 62 percent of delinquents and only 10 percent of nondelinquents disliked school. The metalheads fall in the middle of these two groups (31 percent disliked school). More recently, Stevenson and Stigler (1992) cite studies indicating that 52–65 percent of American middle-school students say they like school, which are lower rates than among Asian students (75–86 percent).

6. Roe (1987; 1990). Also, Gaines (1991) reported that the local vocational and technical school in the suburban town she studied was known as "heavy metal high school" because so many metalheads attended it. This seems to confirm that metalheads prefer a more active, hands-on school environment, where it is available.

Of course, as I note below, not all metalheads hate the college-prep kind of high school. In general a useful distinction can be made between metalheads who are part of the *taste culture* of heavy metal and simply like the high-sensation intensity of the music, and those who are part of the *subculture* of heavy metal, who have in common not just high sensation seeking but also alienation, from school as well as other sources. For those who are part of the subculture, the music is something more serious and essential, more ideological. My sample included boys who were part of the taste culture as well as boys who were part of the subculture; throughout the book I have sought to provide examples of each. See Arnett (1993) and Lull (1987) for further discussion of this distinction.

7. Larson and Richards (1994), p. 89.

8. Durkheim (1915).

9. The statistics that follow are from Gallup and Castelli (1989).

10. For comparison, in a Gallup poll published March 5, 1993, only 4 percent of the American general public identified themselves as agnostics or atheists. However, the fact that 96 percent of Americans say they "believe in God" does not necessarily contradict what I said above about the decline of religious socialization. Agreeing with such an open statement can mean many things to many people, and I would argue that the other information I present here suggests that the role of religion in American society is declining.

11. See Reiff (1966) on what he calls "the triumph of the therapeutic" in American life, including in religion.

12. His skepticism about organized religion is shared by many other adolescents. In a national poll by Gallup and Poling (1980), only 25 percent of adolescents said they had a high degree of confidence in organized religion.

13. See Roof (1993).

14. See Gaines (1991) for further comments and examples in this vein.

Chapter 8

1. This chapter is based on data from 38 female metalheads. Twenty-five of them volunteered after seeing a sign describing the study at a music store; ten of these girls lived in greater Atlanta, Georgia, and 15 lived in greater Boston, Massachusetts. All 25 of these girls were interviewed by female research assistants and completed the same questionnaires as the boys. The other 13 were girls who indicated that they "strongly like" heavy metal on a questionnaire about musical preferences when the data for a comparison group of girls were being collected from the same high school and college as the boys' comparison group. These 13 girls were not interviewed. There were 199 girls in the comparison group.

2. Female metalheads reported higher sensation seeking on the total Sensation-Seeking Scale (p < .01).

3. See Walser (1993) for a description of the male orientation of heavy metal, Brake (1985) for a discussion of male domination of youth subcultures more generally.

4. On the Offer Self-Image Questionnaire (Offer, Ostrov, and Howard, 1982) used in the study, female metalheads reported significantly poorer family relationships than girls in the comparison group on the total scale (p < .001).

5. Although males are generally higher in sensation seeking than females (which partly explains the greater appeal of heavy metal for boys), adolescent girls are generally higher in sensation seeking than their parents (Arnett, 1994).

6. Forty-four percent of the female metalheads described themselves as agnostics or atheists, compared to 22 percent of the girls in the comparison group. However, even this overstates the religiosity of the metalhead girls. As the following examples illustrate, even for those who believe in God, their beliefs are often quite unorthodox, and they generally reject organized religion.

7. In their individualistic approach to religion and their rejection of organized religion, both male and female metalheads sound remarkably similar to many of the baby boomers described by Roof (1993). This makes sense; many of today's metalheads are the children of boomers, and they have grown up in a culture where many people are skeptical of or hostile to organized religion.

8. However, in the same way that male metalheads are more reckless than male nonmetalheads, female metalheads are generally more reckless than girls who do not like heavy metal. They report significantly higher rates of marijuana use, sex without contraception, shoplifting, and vandalism. See Arnett (1991a) for details.

9. Brake (1985).

10. For example, Tanner (1981).

11. Arnett (1994).

Chapter 9

1. Berger and Berger (1984) use the term "hyperindividualism" to refer to an extreme and corrosive form of individualism.

2. Spiro (1994); Wrong (1994).

3. Not, of course, for the African slaves or the Native Americans who were being displaced.

4. For a recent statement of this ideal, see Lifton (1993).

5. For example, Gaines (1991).

6. See Schlegel and Barry (1991) for an interesting anthropological survey of adolescence cross-culturally.

7. "Love and work" was Freud's terse answer when he was asked what an adult should be able to do well in order to be considered psychologically healthy (quoted in Erikson, 1963). I think he was right and that it applies across cultures.

8. Although the "love and work" requirements apply across cultures, the specification that love be expressed in a monogamous, intimate, heterosexual relationship is more specific to contemporary Western cultures. However, it is appropriate to discuss it in this way here, since the American majority culture to which the metalheads belong is one of the cultures in which this ideal of love is found.

9. Erikson (1963).

10. See Becker (1973) for a powerful statement of this thesis.

11. Larson and Richards (1994).

12. Whiting and Edwards (1988).

13. Munroe et al. (1983).

14. Larson and Richards (1994).

15. Ironically, adolescents in these cultures do not by any means have equal status with their parents, even though they contribute near-equal work. An age hierarchy remains throughout life, as in the Indian example described in Chapter 6.

16. Bellah et al. (1985).

references

Alwin, D. F. (1988). "From Obedience to Autonomy: Changes in Traits Desired in Children, 1924–1978." *Public Opinion Quarterly* 52, 33–52.

Alwin, D. F., X. Xu, and T. Carson. (1994). "Child-Rearing Goals and Child Discipline." Paper presented at the Public World of Childhood Project workshop on "Children Harmed and Harmful," October, Chicago.

Armstrong, K. (1993). *A History of God: The 4,000-Year Quest of Judaism, Christianity, and Islam.* New York: Knopf.

Arnett, J. (1991a). "Heavy Metal Music and Reckless Behavior Among Adolescents." *Journal of Youth and Adolescence* 20, 573–592.

———. (1991b). "Adolescents and Heavy Metal Music: From the Mouths of Metalheads." *Youth and Society* 23, 76–98.

———. (1992a). "Reckless Behavior in Adolescence: A Developmental Perspective." *Developmental Review* 12, 339–373.

———. (1992b). "Socialization and Adolescent Reckless Behavior: A Reply to Jessor." *Developmental Review* 12, 391–409.

———. (1992c). "The Soundtrack of Recklessness: Musical Preferences and Reckless Behavior Among Adolescents." *Journal of Adolescent Research* 7, 313–331.

———. (1993). "Three Profiles of Heavy Metal Fans: A Taste for Sensation and a Subculture of Alienation." *Qualitative Sociology* 16, 423–443.

———. (1994). "Sensation Seeking: A New Conceptualization and a New Scale." *Personality and Individual Differences* 16, 289–296.

———. (1995a). "Broad and Narrow Socialization: The Family in the Context of a Multi-Dimensional Theory." *Journal of Marriage and the Family* 57, 617–628.

———. (1995b). "Adolescents' Uses of Media for Self-Socialization." *Journal of Youth and Adolescence* 24, 519–533.

Arnett, J., and L. Balle-Jensen. (1993). "Cultural Bases of Risk Behavior: Danish Adolescents." *Child Development* 64, 1842–1855.

Arnett, J. J., and L. A. Jensen. (1994). "Socialization and Risk Behavior in Two Countries, Denmark and the U.S." *Youth and Society* 26, 3–22.

Arnett, J., and S. Taber. (1994). "Adolescence Terminable and Interminable: When Does Adolescence End?" *Journal of Youth and Adolescence* 23, 517–537.

Becker, E. (1973). *The Denial of Death.* New York: Free Press.

Bellah, R. N., R. Madsen, W. M. Sullivan, A. Swidler, and S. M. Tipton. (1985). *Habits of the Heart: Individualism and Commitment in American Life.* New York: Harper and Row.

Berger, B., and P. L Berger. (1984). *The War over the Family.* New York: Anchor Doubleday.

Brake, M. (1985). *Comparative Youth Culture: The Sociology of Youth Cultures and Youth Subcultures in America, Britain, and Canada.* London: Routledge and Kegan Paul.

Bronfenbrenner, U. (1979). *The Ecology of Human Development.* Cambridge, Mass.: Harvard University Press.

Csikszentmihalyi, M., and R. Larson. (1984). *Being Adolescent: Conflict and Growth in the Teenage Years*. New York: Basic Books.

Davis, S. S., and D. A. Davis. (1989). *Adolescence in a Moroccan Town*. New Brunswick, N.J.: Rutgers University Press.

Demo, D., and A. C. Aycock. (1988). "The Impact of Divorce on Children." *Journal of Marriage and the Family* 50, 619–648.

Durkheim, E. (1897/1951). *Suicide*. New York: Free Press.

Elder Jr., G. H. (1987). "Adolescence in Historical Perspective," in H. J. Graff (ed.), *Growing Up in America: Historical Experiences*. Detroit: Wayne University Press.

Elkind, D. (1967). "Egocentrism in Adolescence." *Child Development* 38, 1025–1034.

———. (1985). "Egocentrism Redux." *Developmental Review* 5, 218–226.

Epstein, J. S., and D. J. Pratto. (1990). "Heavy Metal Rock Music: Juvenile Delinquency and Satanic Identification." *Popular Music and Society* 14, 67–76.

Epstein, J. S., D. J. Pratto, and J. K. Skipper. (1990). "Teenagers, Behavioral Problems, and Preferences for Heavy Metal and Rap Music: A Case Study of a Southern Middle School." *Deviant Behavior* 11, 381–394.

Erikson, E. (1963). *Childhood and Society*, 2d ed. New York: W. W. Norton.

Feldman, S. S., and G. R. Elliott. (1990). "Progress and Promise of Research on Adolescence," in S. S. Feldman and G. R. Elliott (eds.), *At the Threshold: The Developing Adolescent*. Cambridge: Harvard University Press, pp. 479–508.

Fergusson, F. (1961). *Aristotle's Poetics*. New York: Hill and Wang.

Gaines, D. (1991). *Teenage Wasteland: Suburbia's Dead-End Kids*. New York: HarperCollins.

Gallup Jr., G., and J. Castelli. (1989). *The People's Religion: American Faith in the '90's*. New York: MacMillan.

Gallup Jr., G., and D. Poling. (1980). *The Search for America's Faith*. New York: Abington.

Gans, H. (1974). *Popular Culture and High Culture*. New York: Basic Books.

Gilmore, D. (1991). *Manhood in the Making: Cultural Concepts of Masculinity*. New Haven: Yale University Press.

Glueck, S., and E. T. Glueck. (1950). *Unraveling Juvenile Delinquency*. Cambridge: Harvard University Press.

Gober, P. (1993). "Americans on the Move." *Population Bulletin* 48(3). Washington, D.C.: Population Reference Bureau.

Hebdige, D. (1979). *Subculture: The Meaning of Style*. New York: Methuen.

Herdt, G. (1987). *The Sambia: Ritual and Gender in New Guinea*. New York: Holt, Rinehart, and Winston.

Hetherington, E. M. (1991). "The Role of Individual Differences and Family Relationships in Coping with Divorce and Remarriage," in P. A. Cowan and E. M. Hetherington (eds.), *Family Transitions*. Hillsdale, N.J.: Erlbaum.

Holinger, P. C., and D. Offer. (1989). "Risk Factors for Youth Suicide: Sociodemographic, Epidemiological, and Individual Attributes," in L. Davidson and M. Linnoila (eds.), vol. 2, *Report of the Secretary's Task Force on Youth Suicide*. Washington, D.C.: U.S. Department of Health and Human Services, ADAMHA, pp. 19–33.

Horowitz, H. L. (1987). *Campus Life*. New York: Alfred A. Knopf.

James, W. (1902/1961). *The Varieties of Religious Experience.* New York: W. W. Norton.

Jonah, B. A. (1986). "Accident Risk and Risk-Taking Behaviour Among Young Drivers." *Accident Analysis and Prevention* 18, 255–271.

Kaplan, E. A. (1987). *Rocking Around the Clock: Music Television, Postmodernism, and Consumer Culture.* New York: Methuen.

Katz, J. (1982). *Seductions of Crime: Moral and Sensual Attractions of Doing Evil.* New York: Basic Books.

King, P. (1988). "Heavy Metal Music and Drug Abuse in Adolescents." *Postgraduate Medicine* 83, 295–304.

Kohn, M. L. (1977). *Class and Conformity: A Study in Values,* 2d ed. Chicago: University of Chicago Press.

Kurdek, L. (1987). "Gender Differences in the Psychological, Symptomatology, and Coping Strategies of Young Adolescents." *Journal of Early Adolescence* 7, 395–410.

Larson, R., and M. H. Richards. (1994). *Divergent Realities: The Emotional Lives of Mothers, Fathers, and Adolescents.* New York: Basic Books.

Lasch, C. (1979). *Haven in a Heartless World.* New York: Basic Books.

Lewis, G. (1987). "Patterns of Meaning and Choice: Taste Cultures in Popular Music," in J. Lull (ed.), *Popular Music and Communication.* Beverly Hills, Calif.: Sage, pp. 198–211.

Lifton, R. (1993). *The Protean Self: Human Resilience in an Age of Fragmentation.* New York: Basic Books.

Linney, J. A., and E. Seidman. (1989). "The Future of Schooling." *American Psychologist* 44, 336–340.

Lull, J. (1987). "Listeners' Communicative Uses of Popular Music," in J. Lull (ed.), *Popular Music and Communication.* Beverly Hills, Calif.: Sage, pp. 140–174.

Moore, D., and N. R. Schultz. (1983). "Loneliness at Adolescence: Correlates, Attributes, and Coping." *Journal of Youth and Adolescence* 12, 95–100.

Munroe, R. H., R. L. Munroe, C. Michelson, A. Koel, R. Bolton, and C. Bolton. (1983). "Time Allocation in Four Societies." *Ethnology* 22, 355–370.

Offer, D., E. Ostrov, and K. Howard. (1982). "The Offer Self-Image Questionnaire for Adolescents." Chicago: Michael Reese Hospital and Medical Center.

Pattison, R. (1987). *The Triumph of Vulgarity: Rock Music in the Mirror of Romanticism.* New York: Oxford University Press.

Piaget, J. (1967). *Six Psychological Studies.* New York: Random House.

Pielke, R. (1986). *You Say You Want a Revolution: Rock Music in American Culture.* Chicago: Nelson-Hall.

Pitman, J. F., and G. Bowen. (1994). "Adolescents on the Move: Adjustment to Family Relocation." *Youth and Society* 25, 371–385.

Postman, N. (1985). *Amusing Ourselves to Death: Public Discourse in the Age of Show Business.* New York: Penguin.

Richards, P., R. A. Berk, and B. Forster. (1979). *Crime as Play: Delinquency in a Middle-Class Suburb.* Cambridge, Mass.: Ballinger.

Rieff, P. (1966). *The Triumph of the Therapeutic: The Uses of Faith After Freud.* New York: Harper and Row.

Robinson, D. C., E. B. Buck, and M. Cuthbert. (1991). *Music at the Margins: Popular Music and Cultural Diversity.* London: Sage.

Roe, K. (1987). "The School and Music in Adolescent Socialization," in J. Lull (ed.), *Popular Music and Communication.* Beverly Hills, Calif.: Sage, pp. 212–230.

———. (1990). "Adolescents' Music Use: A Structural-Cultural Approach," in K. Roe and U. Carlsson (eds.), *Popular Music Research.* Gothenburg, Sweden: NORDICOM, pp. 41–52.

Roland, A. (1988). *In Search of Self in India and Japan.* Princeton, N.J.: Princeton University Press.

Roof, W. C. (1993). *A Generation of Seekers: The Spiritual Journeys of the Baby Boom Generation.* San Francisco: HarperSanFrancisco.

Rubin, A. M. (1994). "Media Uses and Effects: A Uses-and-Gratifications Perspective," in J. Bryant and D. Zillman (eds.), *Media Effects: Advances in Theory and Research.* Hillsdale, N.J.: Erlbaum, pp. 417–436.

Santrock, J. W., K. A. Sitterle, and R. A. Warshak. (1988). "Parent-Child Relationships in Stepfather Families," in P. Bronstein and C. Cowan (eds.), *The Father's Role Today: Men's Changing Roles in the Family.* New York: Wiley.

Schlegel, A., and H. Barry III. (1991). *Adolescence: An Anthropological Inquiry.* New York: Free Press.

Spencer, P. (1965). *The Samburu: A Study of Gerontocracy in a Nomadic Tribe.* Berkeley: University of California Press.

———. (1973). *Nomads in Alliance: Symbiosis and Growth Among the Rendille and Samburu of Kenya.* London: Oxford University Press.

Spiro, M. E. (1994). *Culture and Human Nature.* New Brunswick, N.J.: Transaction.

Stevenson, H. W., and J. W. Stigler. (1992). *The Learning Gap: Why Our Schools Are Failing and What We Can Learn from Japanese and Chinese Education.* New York: Touchstone.

Sugerman, D. (1991). *Appetite for Destruction: The Days of Guns N' Roses.* New York: St. Martin's Press.

Tanner, J. (1981). "Popular Music and Peer Groups: A Study of Canadian High School Students' Responses to Pop Music." *Canadian Review of Sociology and Anthropology* 18, 1–13.

Turnbull, C. (1962). *The Forest People.* Garden City, New York: Doubleday.

Udry, J. R. (1988). "Biological Predispositions and Social Control in Adolescent Sexual Behavior." *American Sociological Review* 53, 709–722.

U.S. Congress (1985). *Record Labeling (Senate Hearing 99–529): Hearing Before the Committee on Commerce, Science, and Transportation.* U.S. Senate, 99th Cong., 1st sess., on contents of music and the lyrics of records. Washington, D.C.: U.S. Government Printing Office.

U.S. Department of Education (1988). *Youth Indicators 1988: Trends in the Well-Being of American Youth.* (DE Publication No. 065-000-00347-3). Washington, D.C.: U.S. Government Printing Office.

Walser, R. (1993). *Running with the Devil: Power, Gender, and Madness in Heavy Metal Music.* Hanover, N.H.: University Press of New England.

Waters, E., and V. J. Crandall. (1964). "Social Class and Observed Maternal Behavior from 1940 to 1960." *Child Development* 35, 1021–1032.

Weinstein, D. (1991). *Heavy Metal: A Cultural Sociology.* New York: Lexington.

Whitfield, R. A., and D. Fife. (1987). "Changing Patterns in Motor Vehicle Crash Mortality: 1940–1980." *Accident Analysis and Prevention* 19, 261–269.

Whiting, B. B., and C. P. Edwards. (1988). *Children of Different Worlds: The Formation of Social Behavior.* Cambridge: Harvard University Press.

Williams, A. F. (1985). "Nighttime Driving and Fatal Crash Involvement of Teenagers." *Accident Analysis and Prevention* 17, 1–5.

Wilson, J. Q., and R. J. Herrnstein. (1985). *Crime and Human Nature.* New York: Simon and Schuster.

Wrong, D. H. (1994). *The Problem of Order: What Unites and Divides Society.* New York: Free Press.

Zuckerman, M., S.B.G. Eysenck, and H. J. Eysenck. (1978). "Sensation Seeking in England and America: Cross-Cultural, Age, and Sex Comparisons." *Journal of Consulting and Clinical Psychology* 46, 139–149.

about the book and author

Heavy metal is a violent, head-banging music complete, in its live performances, with its own arena of rage and celebration, the slamdancing pit. It is a music in the red corner of society, loud, angry, and, to most adult ears, practically intolerable. And yet, the art form radiates a message about American adolescents well worth examining and comprehending: Its devotees, primarily adolescent boys, are alienated from their world and angry about its future. Heavy metal speaks throbbingly the message of rage, loneliness, and cynicism.

In this sensitive book, Jeffrey Jensen Arnett synthesizes the stories and experiences of seventy male and thirty-eight female "metalheads" in a successful attempt to understand the often alienating results of a society that exalts an ever more extreme individualism. The vacuum such an atmosphere creates in the individual can be temporarily obliterated by a heavy metal concert, which Arnett sees as a substitute manhood ritual. This conclusion is just one of the many striking hypotheses the author advances in this dynamic study of a music and its followers.

Of the more than one hundred metalheads interviewed for this volume, nine are featured in the profiles preceding each chapter—the reader becomes fully acquainted with Jack, for instance, and with the multiple crosses decorating his body, his black rose tattoo, and his tumultuous family life; and with slim and well-groomed Jean, dressed entirely in black, her favorite color, and wearing the temperament of withdrawal.

This is a unique study filled with compassion for a disenfranchised subculture and the respect of a desire to understand it.

Jeffrey Jensen Arnett is associate professor of human development and family studies at the University of Missouri at Columbia.

index

Adolescence, 3, 4, 12–13, 27, 105
  Danish adolescents, 179(n13)
  grandiosity of thinking, 85
  and household duties, 162–163
  and ritual, 15–18
  Swedish adolescents, 121
Advertising, 105
Aggression, 25, 45, 74, 83, 84, 87
  and socialization, 89
  See also Anger
Alcoholism, 21, 36, 103, 136
Alcohol use, 46, 77, 105, 151. See also
  Automobiles, driving intoxicated
Alienation, 1, 3, 4, 10–11, 17, 23, 24, 33,
    34, 41, 44–45, 51, 56, 77, 87, 94, 165,
    180(n16)
  and family/community, 97–110
  future of adolescent, 166–168
  of girls, 137, 139, 143–145, 145–148
  ideology of, 28, 64, 68–71, 155
  meaning of, 17
  and school/religion, 117–133
  sources of, 97–110, 156–157,
    173(n9)
Anger, 4, 20, 30, 41, 45, 53
  purging of, 3, 19, 25, 49, 55, 74,
    81–83, 87, 89, 146
  sources of, 81, 110
Angst, 50, 51, 57, 110
Anthrax, 7, 9, 44
Anxiety, 81, 82
Apocalypse (game), 35
"Architecture of Aggression," 47–48
Aristotle, 41, 56, 176(n18), 178(n9)
Art, 41, 56–57
  vulgar, 57
"At Dawn They Sleep," 52
Atheism, 123, 144, 181(n10)
Authenticity, 127. See also under Heavy
    metal songs/music; Metalheads
Authority, 100, 101, 102, 121

Automatic writing, 93–94
Automobiles
  accident fatalities, 15–16, 24, 79,
    172(n6)
  driving intoxicated, 16, 21, 78
  reckless driving, 21, 79, 173(n17)
  See also Summary profiles

Baby boomers, 182(n7)
"Beavis and Butthead," 23
Becker, Ernest, 77, 117
Bellah, Robert, 23, 166
Black magic, 91, 107. See also
    Satanism
Blacks, 111
Black Sabbath, 43
Blake, William, 63
"Bloodbath in Paradise," 49
"Bodily Dismemberment," 37, 82
Bon Jovi, 70
Boredom, 29
"Born to Be Wild," 43
Brake, Michael, 139
Bronfenbrenner, Urie, 97

"Can I Play with Madness?" 45
Capitalism, 172(n3)
Careers, 137. See also Goals; under
    Heavy metal songs/music
Castelli, Jim, 125, 126
Catharsis, 19
Child molestation, 53
Children, 137, 161–162, 163
Circumcision, 13, 16
Cities, 29
Clothes, 1, 8(photo), 9, 28, 59, 71, 91,
    135, 142
Cocaine, 151
Commercialism, 43, 70, 71, 127, 147
Community, 25, 26, 29–30, 99, 105, 106,
    107–108, 109, 133, 161

Printed in the United Kingdom
by Lightning Source UK Ltd.
102506UKS00004B/157-171